Dear Ernie:

How we missed you at The November 4 gala. But you will always be loved and remembered by the Raclin School of the Arts — and indeed by all of IUSB.

Lester

November 1 2010

A CAMPUS BECOMING

Lester M. Wolfson
and Indiana University South Bend
1964 - 1987

A CAMPUS BECOMING

LESTER M. WOLFSON
AND INDIANA UNIVERSITY SOUTH BEND
1964 - 1987

PATRICK J. FURLONG
TOM R. VANDER VEN

WP
WOLFSON PRESS • SOUTH BEND, IN

Wolfson Press gratefully acknowledges
that publication of this book is supported in part
by a contribution from George Wolfson. Photographs,
illustrations, and some texts are published here courtesy
of the Archives of Indiana University South Bend, and with
the generous assistance of Archivist Alison Stankrauff,
Susan Jacobs, and James Facer. Selections from the writing
of Stephen Spender, John Updike, and Bernard Malamud
are reproduced by permission of the publishers.

Design and editorial team:
David James and Michael Snyder.
Cover design by Cyndi Vander Ven.

ISBN: 978-0-9799532-8-6

Wolfson Press
Master of Liberal Studies Program
Indiana University South Bend
1700 Mishawaka Avenue
South Bend, IN 46634-7111
wolfson.iusb.edu

Table of Contents

Illustrations

Preface

It is right and fitting that this book is being published under the Wolfson Press imprint. It is a book about an institution and a man, the two inextricably entwined. The man, of course, is Lester M. Wolfson, who came to an undernourished South Bend-Mishawaka Campus of Indiana University in 1964 as its director and left the robust Indiana University South Bend in 1987 as its chancellor. The title shifts suggest only the smallest portion of what changed during those years. The campus he found when he arrived offered no degree programs and boasted a full-time faculty numbering just 21, and that included himself. This book describes how the school became the envied model of a regional campus.

I had the privilege of serving as an assistant to Les for 14 years of his nearly two and a half decades as its leader. That was a crucial time in IUSB's coming of age, a period in which, as Les liked to paraphrase a friend at another of IU's regional campuses, IUSB was "evolving into the kind of entity it was inevitably destined to become." He spoke with humor, but in fact there was no inevitability about IUSB's development. Under a leader less devoted to the ideal of a university, it might easily have become a place offering more career courses and fewer of the core disciplines that define a university, as, indeed, even some of his own faculty might have preferred.

Les's notion of higher education was epigrammatic but comprehensive. He once called it "a journey to the light," and he knew that journey must involve the humanities, music, and the arts in addition to skills more narrowly aimed at "a better fit between college training and available vocations," as an internal IU document once put it.

This book, the sixth in the Wolfson Press catalogue, is both a history of the Wolfson years at IUSB and a profile of the chancellor. An enlightening history chapter by Pat Furlong traces the challenges, successes, and frustrations attendant upon fleshing out a curriculum worthy of the name *university*. Tom Vander Ven's profile brings his subject to vibrant life as a man erudite but never stuffy, firm in the pursuit of goals but always open to reason, introspective but uncannily articulate, and above all exquisitely literate—all delivered in Tom's enviable prose.

The rest of the book is devoted to a selection of Les's public addresses, including several "State of the Campus" remarks delivered at fall faculty meetings and some of the commencement addresses he delivered at graduation ceremonies. Cumulatively, they add up to a revealing glimpse of a remarkable mind and spirit at work.

"No one knows better than University people," Les cautioned in one faculty address, "that history is not the lengthened shadow of one man but . . . the happy confluence of many contributing streams of mind and heart." That's undeniable, but in this case, at least, the institution truly is the lengthening shadow of my friend and ex-boss, Lester M. Wolfson.

Walton R. Collins
October 2010

Lester M. Wolfson

A Regional Campus, a Beckoning Ideal

Patrick J. Furlong

Indiana University opened its most northerly outpost in 1933, offering a few evening classes at Central High School in downtown South Bend. The purpose of this "extension center" was simple enough. Local residents who lacked time and money to enroll at the "real" IU campus amid the scenic hills of southern Indiana could take a few freshman and sophomore classes while living at home, and then somehow, someday, journey to Bloomington for two or three years in order to complete their degrees. Few of them ever did so, and IU made no effort to keep track of their numbers. By the middle of the prosperous 1950s the various IU extension centers were elevated to the more noble designation of "regional campuses," but they remained in fact extension centers, offering only freshman and sophomore courses for transfer to Bloomington. They were then and remain today, except for Indianapolis, regional campuses, most emphatically not "branch campuses" on the well-known example of the University of California, which opened a "Southern Branch" in 1919 and renamed it University of California at Los Angeles in 1927. Almost immediately students, faculty, and local journalists began to call it UCLA, just as years later their counterparts in South Bend created IUSB as soon as they had the opportunity.[1] Indiana has never published any public document remotely resembling Clark Kerr's famed *Master Plan for Higher Education in California, 1960-1975*. On the other hand, thanks to the foresight and ambition of IU's president, Herman B Wells, by the early 1960s there was in South Bend the beginning of a campus (still offering only courses for transfer), with a fine new building and a remarkable opportunity for a leader with the energy and the vision to shape a new kind of university.

South Bend was deeply depressed, financially and emotionally, when Lester M. Wolfson assumed the office of director of the local Indiana University Center on July 1, 1964. The Studebaker Corporation had closed the city's oldest and largest business just six months earlier, throwing seven thousand middle-aged workers into unemployment—younger workers had been laid off years earlier. Wolfson's full titles as administrative leader were Director and Assistant Dean, and as a faculty member he was an associate professor of English. What most local residents still thought of as "the extension" was officially called the South Bend-Mishawaka Campus of Indiana University, but the "campus" consisted only of a single building opened three years earlier. Wolfson's predecessor as director, Dr. Jack L. Detzler, had been mysteriously removed from his administrative duties and transferred as a faculty member to the downtown center in Indianapolis. No explanation was given for his removal, and, half a century later, the reasons remain unclear. Apparently the expanding program in South Bend had grown beyond Detzler's abilities to lead, although he retained his position as a tenured faculty member in History. Wolfson was fortunate that the IU leadership in Bloomington transferred Detzler to another campus. He did not stay long in Indianapolis, returning to his hometown to assume a faculty position at Saint Mary's College. Until his death in 2005, Detzler refused further contact with Indiana University.

IU's South Bend center enjoyed a new building on the northern bank of the St. Joseph River, constructed of Indiana limestone to benefit the declining fortunes of the quarries near Bloomington. Previously, most classes were taught by moonlighting high school teachers, and not until 1940 was there a resident director, when Lynton Keith Caldwell, then a University of Chicago graduate student, was named "executive secretary." Dr. Donald F. Carmony headed the extension center from 1944 until 1950, when he was promoted to the home campus in Bloomington. Enrollment reached more than a thousand credit students in 1947-1948 during the full impact of the G.I. Bill, and then declined by 25 per cent before returning to 1,025 in the fall of 1954. Space limitations and insufficient faculty restricted growth until the opening of the IU Center on Northside Boulevard in September of 1961, although there were rapid increases in the numbers of non-credit students in the very active Continuing Education program. By 1961 there were 1,565 credit students and nearly 4,000 non-credit enrollments but only 15 full-time faculty, including the director. Most classes, both credit and non-credit, were taught by adjunct faculty, numbering about one hundred. The new building brought improved

Ground breaking for South Bend–Mishawaka Center (Northside Hall), June 17, 1959. L-R: Paul Gilbert, Committee of 100; Roy Worden, Architect; Dr. Herman B Wells, Indiana University President; Dr. Jack Detzler, Director, South Bend – Mishawaka Center; Mayor Edward F. Voorde, South Bend; not identified.

visibility for IU in South Bend, as well as a rapidly expanding program. In the first semester of the Wolfson administration, in the fall of 1964, there were 2,028 students and a full-time faculty of 21 (including Wolfson), plus 120 adjuncts.

Indiana University's "regional campuses" (as they were known officially by the late 1950s) were only one element of President Herman B Wells's grand vision for Indiana University. In his 1938 inaugural address, Wells referred briefly to the University's responsibility "to supply educational opportunities for adults," including "extension classes off the campus in the evening hours." He made no other reference to the existing extension centers.[2] Although Herman Wells was a leader with a grand vision for Indiana University, his imagination rarely stretched beyond Bloomington and the medical campus in Indianapolis. The "extension centers" in Gary and Fort Wayne had originated as Depression-era junior colleges under the auspices of the local school systems, while South Bend was an IU operation from its beginnings, although in cooperation with the city's school system. There was never a master plan for the extension program, rather a vague dream for providing freshman and sophomore classes for students who could not afford full-time attendance in distant Bloomington.

By the mid-1950s, President Wells, in quiet cooperation with President Frederick L. Hovde of Purdue University, devised a plan to forestall the development of a junior college system for Indiana. Privately, however, Wells described IU's nine extension centers and Purdue's four as the functional equivalents of a junior or community college, offering freshman and sophomore classes, primarily for local and commuting students. Under independent control, such institutions, Wells said, "nearly unavoidably" yield to "local pride, academic competitiveness, and the ambitions which are 'human nature'" and so change "gradually but surely into four-year, collegiate-type of institutions." As Wells put the matter in 1960, when extension centers were already under construction in Gary, Fort Wayne, and South Bend, "If a two-year institution is what is really wanted . . . it is more appropriate in my judgment to let the junior or community college be an extension of an institution of higher learning. . . . If the students . . . are to be students at a *college*, they should study and grow in an atmosphere which is *collegiate*." Facilities and programs would be improved and expanded, but Herman Wells was firmly opposed to four-year degree programs for the regional campuses of Indiana University. A change of policy would come only after his retirement.[3]

The IU extension centers in South Bend, Gary, and Fort Wayne, and later in Kokomo and New Albany, would move from their inadequate, rented buildings into newly-built "Indiana University Centers." The South Bend-Mishawaka Center would be erected on a riverfront site along Northside Boulevard, about a mile east of downtown South

Bend. Wells presided at the ground-breaking ceremony in June of 1959. Seven speakers were listed for the occasion, but the center director was not among them. There would be a single structure, with neither space nor plans for later expansion. The three original centers all featured classrooms and laboratories for lower-level classes only, together with a limited number of offices for full-time faculty and no provision for the large numbers of adjunct faculty who continued to :ach most of the classes. The South-Bend Mishawaka Center had 22 classrooms,

Construction of South Bend-Mishawaka Center (Northside Hall), 1959

laboratories and art studios, but only 14 faculty offices. There were three classrooms for large lecture sections, but no seminar rooms.

There were dreams—pipe dreams really—of full-time Bloomington professors flying across the state to teach classes in the extension centers, but the University had neither the aircraft nor the money to make this a reality. In any event, the distances involved and the often-difficult winter flying conditions in the northern part of the state, in an era before radar or instrument landing systems, would have made such travel exceedingly difficult. The centers had neither cafeterias nor any provision for student recreation of any kind, and their libraries were tiny (and inter-library loan had not yet been invented). Each of the centers did feature a fully-equipped auditorium with a large stage, elaborate lighting, as well as a convenient loading dock for trucks hauling sets and equipment from Bloomington. There were six private dressing rooms at South Bend (apparently never used as such) and two large dressing rooms designated "Men's Chorus" and "Women's Chorus" (which are still used regularly). IU would provide music and theater for the neglected hinterlands, as well as facilities which could be rented at modest cost by community groups. For the formal dedication of the South Bend-Mishawaka Center, the entire Indiana University Opera Orchestra traveled from Bloomington to provide the music, featuring works of Puccini, Verdi, and Mozart.[4] Unfortunately the architects

The original marquee on Northside Hall

for the Center, later named Northside Hall, designed an 800-seat house for the professionally-sized stage, making it almost impossible to seat a large enough audience to cover the cost of bringing casts, crew, and sets from Bloomington. The auditorium lobby, at the main entrance to the building, faced the St. Joseph River across Northside Boulevard. Parking for patrons, however, was at the far end of the building, and access was by way of corridors which a half-century later are still unmarked for visitors. Lester Wolfson would have to find some way to make use of this facility in ways entirely unforeseen by those who designed it.

Lester M. Wolfson Takes Charge

When the IU Center in South Bend opened in the fall of 1961, the chief administrative officer was Jack Detzler, with the title of Director and Assistant Dean. Detzler was a South Bend native who completed his Ph.D. in history at Indiana University in 1952, two years after he was named director of the extension center then located at Central High School. Detzler was an uninspiring leader as well as an ineffective public speaker, and, during his fourteen years as director, accomplished little. He seems to have had little influence in the location of the campus or the design of the new building, and he never became a significant public figure in the community. For reasons which do not appear in the record, he was removed from his position in the spring of 1964. Apparently this was the result of accumulated frustrations among the leadership of the Extension Division, particularly Dean Smith Higgins and Associate Dean Rufus Reiberg, although the final decision was made by President Wells. Detzler had no further connection with Indiana University, and left no files, no plans, and no advice for his successor. There was no "transition" of leadership—in fact Detzler departed without speaking a word to Wolfson.

The incoming director "inherited" an almost-new building, but not yet a campus—a growing enrollment—a small but growing full-time faculty—a limited curriculum with no degree programs and little structure for transfer programs. There was as yet no national model for "regional campuses" within a state university system. Clark Kerr's California plan was very different—a multi-campus research university with an array of doctoral programs and rigorous admission standards, a dozen or so state colleges with masters-degree programs and less rigorous admissions standards, and a large number of junior colleges offering both transfer and terminal programs and a policy of open admission for any high school graduate. Indiana University would be something quite different, uneasily sharing state appropriations with Purdue University, both determined to prevent the growth of a state system of junior colleges by establishing "regional campuses" in population centers to provide wider opportunities, but supposedly of the same quality and the same admission standards as the traditional residential campuses in Bloomington and West Lafayette. Both universities maintained small but separate extension centers in Indian-apolis, which offered limited opportunities for residents of the state's largest city. Within these institutional limits and with improved but still very much limited funding, Wolfson was free to shape a small campus to a new model. His choice, and it was certainly a conscious choice, envisioned a small-scale university much like the Herman Wells's ideal for the Bloomington campus: at its heart would be the traditional liberal arts, expanded to include music and theater, with sciences in a secondary role for financial reasons, and programs in Business and Education to meet the vocational demands of students and community leaders. Logically, in the industrial city of South Bend there should also have been engineering courses, but engineering programs were jealously guarded by Purdue and forbidden to all IU campuses. Herman Wells retired as president in 1962, but his influence remained strong throughout Indiana University for many years, while his two short-term successors, Elvis J. Stahr (1962-1968) and Joseph L. Sutton (1968-1971), showed limited interest in the regional campuses. It was Stahr, however, who presented a grand plan for the administrative reorganization of the entire university to the trustees in April of 1968, including the new office of vice president for regional campuses. The trustees approved his proposals, but three months later Stahr unexpectedly resigned.[5]

The greatest change in the status of IU and Purdue's regional campuses was the result of prolonged academic and political argument on statewide policy for higher education. While the change had great impact in South Bend, local concerns were merely incidental to the wider struggle for degree programs on the regional campuses. A comprehensive study was ordered by the General Assembly in 1963. President Hovde of Purdue advocated publicly-supported four-year degree programs for the four most populous counties of Indiana—Allen, Lake, Marion, and St. Joseph, both to meet local needs and to aid the residential campuses in Bloomington and West Lafayette in dealing with the expected "tidal wave" of students as the first of the baby-boom generation entered college. The decision would be made by the 1965 session of the Indiana General Assembly. Governor Roger Branigan announced that he favored the proposal and recommend-ed an appropriation for $4.1 million for the expansion of programs and facilities at the six IU and Purdue regional campuses in the four counties. In the same budget message, Branigan also recommended a reduction of $18 million in the overall appropriations for the two universities. Regional campus expansion would be cut from funding for the traditional residential campuses, a response to the needs of higher education, some academics would say, to be expected from anti-intellectual Hoosier politicians of the time. After vigorous debate, the legislature approved the governor's recommendation in February, 1965, and at last the South Bend-Mishawaka Campus was authorized to confer bachelor's degrees. At the first South Bend commencement on June 9, 1967, President Elvis Stahr presented diplomas to 31 graduates in Business and Education. Although the first degrees were in "vocational" fields, Wolfson's primary interest was always in the liberal arts. From his arrival in South Bend in 1964 until the serious budget troubles of the early 1970s, Wolfson worked steadily to establish degree programs in the liberal arts and sciences as well as the fine and performing arts which were, to his mind, an integral part of the liberal arts. At the same time, this objective necessarily required the recruitment of many new faculty members. Wolfson personally interviewed every candidate in these early years, and most of the newly hired (largely men in those years) were young graduates from well-regarded research universities. Few came from the Ivy League or the Deep South, many from the larger Midwestern or California universities. Most of them had their new Ph.D. degrees in hand and were appointed as assistant professors; others were hired as lecturers and allowed two or sometimes three years to complete their dissertations. Only a few came from the mother IU campus in Bloomington, and even fewer had sufficient experience for appointment at advanced rank. The faculty was overwhelmingly young and with limited academic experience. When faculty hiring slowed as a result of the financial troubles of the early- and mid-seventies, combined with diminished hiring in the liberal arts nationwide, the result was a cohort of young faculty advancing in age, rank, and tenure, with few newcomers to bring fresh ideas and a spirit of innovation. Several Arts and Sciences departments became completely tenured. The History department, for example, went from 1973 to 1991 without hiring a new full-time faculty member.

Three early faculty appointments deserve particular attention. Robert W. Demaree, his IU dissertation still far from completion, was hired as Lecturer and Director of Music in 1965. Warren Pepperdine, a very recent graduate of the University of Minnesota, was hired in 1965 as assistant professor and director of theater. Gerald E. Harriman, about ten years older and with some years of experience in state government finance, was hired as an associate professor of business in 1966 and soon appointed chairman of the newly-established Division of Business. All three remained until retirement, Demaree and Pepperdine creating a remarkable record of musical and theatrical productions marked, to Wolfson's occasional frustration and the amusement of others not so closely involved, by their prolonged disputes over scheduling use of the auditorium and its spacious stage. After years of a new full-time faculty member first with the ambiguous title of "chairman" and later with the far more appropriate "dean of business of economics," Harriman advanced in August, 1975, to the

Robert W. Demaree

highest academic administrative position at South Bend, known first as dean of faculties, then called vice chancellor for academic affairs. Wolfson rarely concerned himself with the faculty or programs in business, which he left of Harriman's able management. The Division of Education was quite different; there Wolfson struggled for years to find stable and effective leadership. Education had a large enrollment, both graduate and undergraduate, but its curriculum was tightly controlled by the teacher certification regulations of the State Department of Education, as well as through the unwelcome oversight of the School of Education in Bloomington. Its faculty were a frequent cause for worry, with a continuing procession of disputed tenure and promotion decisions.

The Division of Arts and Sciences was established in 1968, to the surprise of most of its faculty, for there was no discussion before the decision was announced. Equally surprising was the appointment of

Warren Pepperdine

Donald D. Snyder as chairman of Arts and Sciences. Snyder, hired only the year before as an associate professor of physics, was at least fifteen years older than most newly-hired faculty, and he had been a tenured faculty member at Andrews University in Berrien Springs, Michigan, about thirty miles north of South Bend. Throughout his twenty-four years with Indiana University, Snyder continued to live in Berrien Springs, never attending evening events on campus or developing any links to community leaders in South Bend, Mishawaka, or Elkhart. Although a man of the highest ethical and moral standards, Snyder proved to be a stubborn and unimaginative chairman and soon became unpopular with many of the Arts and Sciences faculty. He was an almost invisible presence to students, who generally showed little if any interest in these organizational changes which meant so much to the faculty. One year later, the Department of Economics was shifted from Arts and Sciences to Business, hereafter called the Division of Business and Economics. The decision was regretted by most faculty in Arts and Sciences, but welcomed by the economics faculty, who looked forward to enhanced salaries as part of the more prosperous field of business. In this they were soon proved to be correct. Don Snyder made no effort to prevent this grave loss to Arts and Sciences, and seems never to have realized its importance. Despite a long record of faculty frustration, Dr. Snyder remained as chairman, certainly never the leader, of Arts and Sciences until 1978.

Creation of new degree programs was entirely a university responsibility before the establishment of the Indiana Commission for Higher Education in 1971, and rarely a matter of controversy afterwards. The great exception was the request for bachelor's degrees in Music and Music Education. Wolfson was an advocate for music from the start of his administration, and a strong supporter of Robert Demaree, whom he named chairman of Music in 1965. The formal proposal for the creation of the Division of Music was submitted in November of 1968, with the full support of the famed IU School of Music in Bloomington. Wolfson provided John W. Ryan, then vice president for regional campuses, with a clear statement of his vision for the campus in its community context:

> Apart for the obvious mission we have to develop substantial programs in Business and Education, coupled with a careful development in the usual liberal arts areas, it has been clear for some time that a distinctive feature of the South Bend Campus already is—and I hope will continue to be—a development in the various creative and performing arts, particularly as the fine arts relate to the total community. South Bend is a community of extreme devotion to the arts, and our music, drama, and painting programs have already made substantial contributions . . . to our students directly but to the general public as well.[6]

For reasons never clear to anyone at IUSB, the new Commission was decidedly hostile to the Music program at IUSB. Demaree was so frustrated by the delays which extended month after month that he and the entire Music faculty contemplated resignation and public protest to bring pressure on the Commission. "By the time talented faculty and students have departed from IUSB," he told Wolfson in July of 1973, "there need be no final decision, in a commission hearing, on our degree proposals." At last, with strong support from the *South Bend Tribune* and from the central administration of the university, the Higher Ed Commission finally approved Music degrees for both South Bend and Fort Wayne in December, 1973:

> It may be we deserve a moment of euphoria [Demaree told his Music colleagues and friends] . . . An elemental battle has been fought, it seems to me, to determine the boundaries of the university IUSB is becoming. The ground appears to have been well-chosen, and the strategies—the guiding visions and the more recent tactics—successful . . . Now perhaps we can get back to the music.[7]

In 1984 the Commission unanimously approved IUSB's proposal for offering a Master of Music degree. "Thus is ended," said Demaree, "a struggle almost twenty years old this year." He presided over a flourishing Music department, with a fine pianist, a resident string quartet, and as Wolfson fully understood, at least one well-publicized program in which IUSB clearly excelled the University of Notre Dame.

Although Wolfson submitted a *Master Plan for the South Bend-Mishawaka Campus* on March 15, 1966, followed by a revised and enlarged edition on August 15, the document was probably written chiefly in Bloomington. It is remarkable for its impossibly ambitious plans for expansion: a full-time faculty increasing from 87 to 258 over a period of eight years, while the number of bachelor's degree programs would soar from two to 25, and minor subject areas increase from 13 to 34. Administrators would increase modestly, from four to nine, but the clerical and support staff would jump from 26 to 154. Projected overall enrollment would grow from 2,454 in 1965 to 7,027 by 1974, a level not in fact achieved until 1990. Even more remarkable—and unrealistic—was the projected increase in student credit hours, the best overall measure of campus productivity. The 1966 Master Plan reported 20,267 credit hours for the fall of 1965 and estimated 77,297 for the fall of 1974, a level finally achieved in 2009. The mid-1960s were truly a time of academic dreams for the IU regional campus in north central Indiana, pipe dreams to be sure, for even had the predicted horde of students appeared, there was no prospect for facilities or state funding to accommodate them. In retrospect such estimates appear simply fanciful, but for years such calculations, forwarded from Bloomington, made realistic planning almost impossible.

Slower Progress and Tighter Budgets

John Peck from the Division of Business and Economics led the first locally-based effort at long-range planning for IUSB in 1971-72. The Peck Committee made two vital recommendations for new programs, both intended to spur expansion in fields which some faculty believed Wolfson was neglecting: computer science and nursing. The chief problem was not a lack of vision but rather a lack of money, combined in the case of nursing with the difficulty of dealing with a "system school" program, administered from Indianapolis and claiming jurisdiction over all IU campuses. Another system-wide program, the School of Public and Environmental Affairs, established degree programs at IUSB at the direction of central university authorities in 1972. Local faculty and administrators were not involved. The environmental side of SPEA quickly faded away in South Bend, but programs in public administration (previously part of political science) and criminal justice (previously part of sociology) attracted significant numbers of students. Donald Snyder, Chairman of Arts and Sciences, protested vigorously about the diversion of resources and students, to no avail. When SPEA was abolished at IUSB in 2008, both programs returned to Arts and Sciences.

Programs in Dental Hygiene and Dental Assisting came to South Bend in 1969, under the distant supervision of the IU School of Dentistry in Indianapolis. Dental Assisting was a one-year certificate program, while Dental Hygiene was a two-year associate degree program. Both of the dental programs were immediately successful and often reached their enrollment limits, dependent upon the number of dental chairs which could be fitted into the space available in the small Riverside Hall. Of course neither program fitted the self-defined mission of IUSB, but both were well-established IU programs from the Indianapolis campus, and there was no other institutional home for them in the absence of a state community college system. On the other hand, no one ever knew quite what to do with the Division of General and Technical Studies (DGTS), established at Indianapolis in 1965 to provide opportunities for "culturally disadvantaged" students who could not meet the usual IU admission requirements. Suspicious critics believed that DGTS was another IU effort to forestall a junior college system for Indiana. By the early 1970s DGTS was officially "integrated" into the regional campuses, although Chancellor Wolfson and the IUSB faculty showed no enthusiasm for the new program. A few courses were offered, and by 1974 Wolfson was pressured by the central IU administration to hire a DGTS director for South Bend. Samuel Wiersteiner's responsibilities were always vague, as he attempted to direct a program with an uncertain mission, a nominal budget, and no faculty. Not long after his resignation in December, 1979, DGTS faded away on all IU campuses and was soon forgotten. Its mission passed to the new Indiana Vocational Technical College, soon known as IVY Tech, but years would pass before the potential conflicts of mission and state appropriations became a matter of serious concern for the IU regional campuses.

A few computer science classes appeared in the mathematics department's offerings by the late 1960s, but there was no degree program until 1979, when Roland Garrett, chairman of Arts and Sciences, sacrificed geography in order to finance computer science. IUSB already had two geographers, with plans to hire a third and establish a degree program, when the unexpected resignation of one of the geographers created an opportunity to transfer the two vacant budget lines to computer science, which quickly grew into a vital degree program. The lone surviving geographer was shifted into the sociology department and later into SPEA. IUSB has never developed a degree in geography. Remarkably, within a few years, Wolfson became an enthusiastic advocate for computer science. In endorsing a grant application in 1983, he noted that the state had never provided direct financial support for this essential program: "We have re-allocated within our operating budget to provide for the instructional costs," but external support was needed for equipment purchases. In a hand-written note attached to his official letter of support, addressed to William Farquhar of the contract administration office in Bloomington, Wolfson said: "Bill: I know of no other project in my near-20 years at IUSB that I would more emphatically endorse. It would be approaching the tragic if we were to lose the momentum we have gained through extraordinary effort to this point."

Administrative computing came earlier, driven by the need to process student registration and grade reports which as centralized university functions were already computerized. Keypunch machines which could punch and read the once-familiar IBM cards came first, soon linked by a terminal to the central administrative computer at Bloomington using ordinary telephone connections. Donald Snyder, chairman of Arts and Sciences, and Kris Froehlke, head of computer services, such as they were, asked Wolfson for the purchase of a Univac 9200 stand-alone computer for IUSB in the summer of 1970. They estimated the cost at $12,810 for the computer itself, with a total cost (including such peripheral equipment as memory, card punch and card reader machines, and a printer) of $56,269—an impossible amount at that time. A few faculty members were already beginning to ask for computer support for their research projects, increasing from "a few jobs a week at Notre Dame" in 1970 to 25-50 jobs a day through the Bloomington terminal by 1972. Demand increased steadily in both the number and complexity of jobs, and both students and faculty argued that computer service was essential for their research and assignments. Delays were a constant problem, as the central computer system in Bloomington had only 32 ports for remote data access to serve the entire eight-campus IU system. Wolfson himself had little under-standing of computers, but he realized that they had become essential for any modern university and struggled to find money somewhere in a tight budget. By 1980 the IUSB faculty-staff computer com-mittee settled upon a Prime 550 Mod II minicomputer as the most affordable machine for the rapidly growing demand for computer ser-vice at IUSB, although they warned that the standard 80-megabyte disk would probably not provide enough memory. In this they were entirely correct—IUSB eventually purchased ten memory disk units for its miniature "mainframe," with a total capacity of about two giga-bytes before turning to desktop computers in the early 1990s. After prolonged financial delays, IUSB finally signed a lease/purchase agree-ment with the Prime Computer Corporation in September, 1981, at a total cost of $300,721—payable at $5,000 a month over a term of sixty months, including interest at 14 per cent. Before the loan was paid off the Prime 550 was traded in for a much improved Prime 9955, at a total cost of $297,828, payable over five years at an interest rate of 10 per cent. These computers were the largest equipment purchases at IUSB during the Wolfson years, little noticed by most faculty and students, but essential for the growing numbers, especially in Business and the sciences, whose scholarship had become utterly dependent upon computer service. By 1991 every faculty member had a desktop personal computer, while a dozen or so classrooms were converted into computer labs for student use.

The Troubled Development of Nursing at IUSB

The most difficult and persistent curricular and administrative problems occurred with Nursing, a tightly centralized program headquartered in Indianapolis. When established by the IU Board of Trustees as a system school in 1974, its self definition was explicit: "The Indiana University School of Nursing has *one* Baccalaureate Program offered at various geographic locations and is accredited by the National League for Nursing and the Indiana State Board of Nursing."[8] The nursing degree for South Bend was approved in 1979 and, for the remainder of his term as chancellor, Wolfson found himself in almost constant conflict with Elizabeth M. Grossman, the powerful and determined dean of the School of Nursing. Unfortunately for IUSB, the dean usually prevailed over the chancellor, although in theory he held a higher rank in the IU hierarchy.

Creation of a nursing program was complex enough without the problems of a system school. Local hospitals were phasing out their traditional three-year diploma (non-degree) programs for training registered nurses, while universities could offer the baccalaureate RN program only in close cooperation with a nearby hospital for the essential clinical courses. In Indianapolis, of course, there were university-owned hospitals available. In addition, nursing classes required expensive equipment on campus, and there was also an unfunded demand on the already-tight library budget for the purchase of expensive nursing journals and books. Every university struggled during the 1970s to recruit nursing faculty who combined the necessary clinical experience with the newly-required graduate degrees for instructors in baccalaureate programs. In fact, the troubled Director of Nursing at IUSB earned her doctorate in education.

There was no problem finding students interested in nursing, and a good proportion of the nursing faculty completed their graduate degrees after appointment as lecturers. The critical dispute arose from repeated problems in the relations between IUSB and staff and administration at Memorial Hospital, as well as troubles within the nursing program itself. Esther Mooneyhan received consistent and enthusiastic support from Dean Grossman in Indianapolis, who rejected all complaints from Chancellor Wolfson. University policy clearly provided that faculty members in system schools needed both campus and school approval for tenure and promotion. The IUSB promotion and tenure committee, as well as the chancellor, recommended against tenure for Dr. Mooneyhan. Dean Grossman insisted that she receive tenure, and IU president John Ryan forced Wolfson to withdraw his negative recommedation. Dean Grossman agreed that Dr. Mooneyhan would give up her administrative responsibilities, but fourteen months later she reneged on this compromise and restored Dr. Mooneyhan to leadership of the nursing program at IUSB. She would now be called "coordinator" however, and not "director." The administrative conflict between IUSB and the School of Nursing continued, at a lower level of intensity, until Dr. Mooneyhan retired in 1991.

Despite these administrative problems, by 1986-1987 IUSB was able to develop a bachelor's degree program in nursing leading to certification as a registered nurse. At the same time, Memorial Hospital discontinued its own long-established three-year RN program and agreed to provide clinical facilities for IUSB nursing students. During the 1987 session of the General Assembly, a South Bend representative who was the ranking Democratic member of the powerful Ways and Means Committee, B. Patrick Bauer, managed to add $1,000,000 to the biennial appropriation for IUSB to fund the new nursing program. This was the first occasion for which a local representative took such a public role in legislative support for the campus. Indiana University had for many years discouraged faculty and administrators in South Bend from seeking help from local legislators, on the theory that centralized IU efforts would be in the best interests of the university as a whole. As chancellor, Wolfson never dared to challenge this policy, although all of his successors have worked publicly to secure financial and program support from area legislators.

Other New Programs

Neither campus administrators nor a faculty committee suggested a women's studies program. The initiative came from Dr. Gloria K. Shapiro [known as Gloria Kaufman from 1973], a member of English faculty since 1965, who brought to this new cause her remarkable energy and determination. From its beginnings in the mid-1970s, women's studies at IUSB was an interdisciplinary program without a clear institutional structure. Dr. Kaufman received very limited financial support, but she had greater success in winning approval for a number of interdisciplinary courses in women's studies, often before the much larger campuses in Bloomington and Indianapolis. Chancellor Wolfson did not come easily to the support of such an innovative and occasionally controversial program, but he always had strong respect for Dr. Kaufman's intellect and tenacity. By 1981 students were able to earn a minor in Women's Studies, but a degree program was not fully approved until 1999.

Cooperative arrangements between Indiana University and its great rival Purdue University had been discussed by presidents and other high-ranking administrators since the 1950s. The breakthrough was the unification of both universities' various programs in the state's capital in 1969, under the awkward but expressive title of Indiana University-Purdue University-Indianapolis, usually abbreviated IUPUI. For Indianapolis, IU was the dominant partner, while PU controlled the similar arrangement for the combined regional campus in Fort Wayne, known initially as IU-PU-FW, established in 1975, and now called IPFW. Although the importance of manufacturing in South Bend and Mishawaka might seem to have made this a likely location for an extension center offering Purdue's well-regarded engineering and technology programs, Purdue had never shown any interest, although it later established a small regional campus in La Porte County called Purdue North Central. After prolonged negotiations between Bloomington and

West Lafayette, IU and Purdue entered into a "guest-host agree-ment" to locate an Electrical Engineering Technology degree program at IUSB in 1984. Later expanded to include Mechanical Engineering Technology and Organization Leadership, the Purdue programs at IUSB have never attracted large numbers of students.

The non-academic leadership of IUSB was remarkably lean dur-ing the Wolfson years, although some faculty imagined that the campus suffered from an expensive and top-heavy administration. The chief financial officer from 1968 until 1988, called the busi-ness manager, was Otis Romine, a former Studebaker employee and a leader of the St. Joseph County Republican organization. He was a colorful character, often controversial, and frequently unpopular with the administrative hierarchy in Bloomington. Far more popular was Walton R. Collins, who served as Assistant to the Chancellor for University Relations, with responsibility for community relations, publicity, and fund-raising. He was formerly employed as a writer and editor for the *South Bend Tribune*, and he enjoyed a wide range of friends in the community. He worked closely with faculty and with student journalists on *The Preface*, but most of all Walt was a confidant and adviser for the chancellor. He served at IUSB from 1969 until 1983, when he left to become the editor of *Notre Dame Magazine*. His successor was John Sevier, a former sociology professor, who was more active in fund-raising but lacked Walt Collins's talent for dealing with a remarkably wide variety of people.

When John W. Ryan became president of the university in 1971, he named Dr. Sylvia Bowman of the Fort Wayne campus as his replacement as chancellor for regional campuses. She con-tinued the existing policies of micro-management in matters of finance and tenure, to Wolfson's silent frustration. In public, and particularly to the faculty, he was the loyal "organization man" who invariably followed directives from higher authority. Not until Regional Campus Administration (RCA) was abolished in 1974 did the regional chancellors report directly to the president of the university. Ryan allowed them greater financial discretion, but as university president he remained the supreme command-er. Students were almost entirely unaware of these troubles, but many faculty chafed at what they saw as delay and obstruction from the RCA offices in Indianapolis or later the president's office in Bloomington. The most direct challenge to this system came at the initiative of George A. Wing, an energetic

and politically astute professor of business, who held his doctorate from the renowned IU School of Business in Bloomington. The "Ad-Hoc Committee to Examine the Various Aspects of the Indiana University System as It Affects the Future of IUSB" was established by the Academic Senate early in 1974 to investigate and document the ways in which the university under-funded and neglected its regional campuses and their students, in contrast to the residential campus in Bloomington. Wing was always the driving force, but the committee was chaired by a soft-spoken biologist, Earl J. Savage, so that its published findings (October, 1974) became known as the *Savage Committee Report*. The higher administration in Bloomington was suitably outraged and denied the accuracy of the Savage Committee's statistics, even though all of the financial data were taken directly from official university reports to the state government. Wolfson found himself forced to oppose his faculty and support his administrative superiors, but in later years he quietly admitted the accuracy of the Savage Report's criticism of the central administration.

Otis Romine

Expanding the Campus

Planning for the expansion of the campus was another problem that persisted throughout the Wolfson years. Although President Wells and the Extension Division in Bloomington did indeed provide a handsome building for South Bend, they gave little attention to the site itself. It did offer a fine view of the St. Joseph river, although only the auditorium lobby offered a public view of the scene. Northside Boulevard was not a major thoroughfare, and the IU Center lacked public visibility. To the north and west of the campus, along Greenlawn Avenue, there was a small factory, Huckins Tool and Die Works, acquired by the University in 1960 and remodeled for classroom and office use in 1965-66. Now that there were two IU buildings in South Bend it was necessary to find names for them. Buildings on the mother campus were named for donors, such as the Lilly Library, for their function, such as Chemistry, or for some distinguished university leader or professor, such as Bryan Hall. For South Bend the buildings were named for the adjacent streets, and half a century later we still have Northside Hall and Greenlawn Hall, names neither inspiring nor functional. Wolfson apparently selected the names himself, thinking of them as merely temporary. Across Greenlawn Avenue and facing on busy Mishawaka Avenue was the recently erected limestone headquarters of the Associates Investment Co., and behind it the strictly functional red-brick corporate computing center. There seemed to be no hope for IUSB to expand westward. To the east, at the corner of Northside Boulevard and 20th Street, was the St. Joseph County juvenile detention center, which the University managed to obtain only in the late 1990s for development as a parking lot. To the north, beyond the student parking lots, was the Coca-Cola Bottling Plant at the corner of Greenlawn and Mishawaka avenues. Along 20th Street and the remaining Mishawaka Avenue frontage were private homes, which the University gradually purchased and years later demolished to expand the student parking lots.

Increasing enrollments during the late 1960s soon overcrowded the existing buildings. The first remedy, intended as temporary, was the purchase of property along the river occupied by a disreputable nightclub called the Boat Club. It was demolished and replaced by an inexpensive single-story structure for laboratories and faculty offices which was named Riverside Hall (informally known to some as "Riverbottom" Hall). It too was intended as temporary when it opened early in 1970, and it remains in use today as the location of the dental hygiene program.

The most notable expansion during this phase of campus expansion was a massive six-story addition to Northside Hall, originally known as Northside West. Unlike the original handsome limestone structure to which it was attached, Northside West was made of precast concrete panels in order to save on construction costs. The addition, erected in 1970-72, provided greatly needed space for Music, Fine Arts, all of the sciences, and most important, at long last, adequate space for the rapidly-growing library. Because the long-range plan called for early development of a free-standing library in the near future, the new library was considered a temporary tenant. It occupied three floors, with the entrance on the top floor and a single open stairway. There was no elevator for passengers or books. Disabled students had to be led by library staff to the nearby building elevators outside the library, and then admitted to the lower levels by unlocking the alarmed emergency exits. This "temporary" arrangement lasted for 16 years.

A Non-Traditional Pattern of Student Life

There was also prolonged delay in the decision to purchase 26.5 acres of mostly undeveloped land directly across the river from Northside Hall. The owners of the par-3 golf course which occupied most of the site were willing, some would say eager, to sell the land in the early 1970s, but in the absence of a settled long-range plan for campus expansion, the IU real estate office in Bloomington repeatedly ignored what local officials considered an obvious opportunity. It was not until 1994, years after Wolfson's retirement, that IU finally acquired this valuable acreage, the only vacant property adjacent to the campus, except for untouchable city parks. With extensive federal aid, an elegant footbridge across the river connected the separated portions of the campus in 2006. The first long-awaited student housing—denied by University authorities and the Indiana Higher Education Commission for so many years—opened two years later. Long-serving faculty remembered when Chancellor Wolfson had been publicly rebuked by IU President John Ryan for daring to suggest on-campus housing for IUSB students.

The IU regional campuses of the 1960s were part of a new wave in American higher education, enrolling large numbers of what came to be known as "non-traditional" students. Americans had long viewed the "college years" as a time enjoyed by young men and women in their late teens and early twenties, attending school full-time, living in dormitories or fraternity and sorority houses, cheering on the football team on Saturday afternoon. At IUSB, by contrast, the average student was in her late twenties (more than 60 per cent of the students were women), working or raising a family (often both), with neither time, money, nor energy for "college life." There were exceptions, particularly journalists and theater majors who worked together closely as cast members and stage crew, but most IUSB students left campus immediately after class and only reluctantly attended campus events such as plays, concerts, and visiting speakers recommended by the faculty. In marked contrast to such traditional campuses as Bloomington or Ann Arbor, half a century after moving onto its own campus, IUSB to this day cannot support a single neighborhood tavern as a student hangout, although a large proportion of its students are of legal drinking age.

Elaborate master plans and campus expansion studies from the late 1960s well into the 1980s envisaged new academic structures and two or perhaps three multi-level parking facilities to relieve the never-ending student complaints about finding a parking space on campus. These plans usually included some sort of student center, but for many years there was little concern for any social life beyond the classroom for students at IUSB, either from the local administration or from the central university authorities in Bloomington. The original IU Center, later Northside Hall, included a single student lounge with a seating capacity of perhaps 90. The only food service was provided by a few vending machines dispensing coffee, soft drinks, candy, and stale sandwiches. The most popular class period was scheduled for 5:30 p.m., meaning students who came directly from work had no chance for a meal until after class, often after 8:10 p.m. and for some even later. Recreation meant a single ping-pong table. The mother campus in Bloomington provided elaborate facilities for student life: a large and well-furnished student union, three swimming pools, a multitude of tennis courts, even a golf course. Those who attended the regional campuses were "non-residential students" who presumably lived at home and required neither food nor recreation. Tuition rates, remarkably, were until the mid-1970s more expensive for regional campus students, who paid by the credit hour at a higher rate than full-time students in Blooming-ton, who paid a flat fee however many credit hours they attempted. Complaints, however, were few and little noticed, except the everlast-ing student plea for more parking spaces.

One cause which stirred strong feelings among many students as well as a number of young faculty was the provision for child care at IUSB. This was of course a new issue for American higher education in the 1970s, when young parents, both mothers and fathers, called upon employers and universities to make it easier for them to attend or teach classes by providing convenient care for young children. Child care was an entirely new concept for Indiana University and natu-rally of greater interest to the non-traditional students on the regional campuses. Officials at Bloomington were notably lacking in concern for young children. An off-campus Day Care Center was established nearby in 1970, with limited financial assistance from Student Gov-ernment. Wolfson very gradually agreed to support the concept of on-campus child-care, using space available in the University Center Building, part of the property purchased from the Associates Corpo-ration. When the Parents Plus organization lost its rented space from a church on North Ironwood Dr., Wolfson finally allowed child care on campus in 1982. Three years later he formally requested permission from President Ryan to expend university funds to remodel a student lounge for a full-scale child care facility. The IUSB Day Care Center opened in March, 1986, after a sixteen-year campaign by concerned parents, students, staff, and faculty.[9] A flourishing and expanded Child Development Center operates today in the same location.

Surprisingly for those who had attended a traditional residential college or university, the "non-traditional" students of IUSB—some-what older, many employed full-time, many married and parents of young children—showed very little interest in athletics. From the early 1970s, a small number of faculty argued that a basketball team would enhance IUSB's public visibility and attract larger numbers of male students. A women's team was imagined only some years later. A club basketball team was established in 1972, funded through the Student Association and playing in a rented public school gymnasi-um before a "crowd" of several dozen. An eligibility scandal involving non-student players soon ended IUSB's athletic efforts, and a formal athletic program did not emerge until 1986. Wolfson reluctantly gave his consent for "this modest development for sports at IUSB," but he emphatically told the IU vice president for administration "that I will never approve the expenditure of one uncompensated general fund cent for the support of intercollegiate athletics."[10]

IUSB in the Era of Student Unrest and Rebellion

Commuter students were not entirely immune to the student unrest and the anti-war movement of the late 1960s and early 1970s, but protests at South Bend were more likely to be led by young faculty members than by the students, many of whom were older than their teachers. Several incidents attracted public notice and a few complaints about unpatriotic troublemakers, but there was no violence beyond occasional pushing and shoving. There was, however, a good deal of shouting and chanting of slogans. The first "demonstration" occurred around noon on March 14, 1968, as members of the public departed from a highway conference held in the auditorium. Dr. Kenneth Lux, a young faculty member in psychology, who had submitted his resignation a few days earlier, led a Students for a Democratic Society [SDS] anti-war protest carrying an American flag to which he had attached a picture of the Cuban revolutionary hero Che Guevara. A few aroused guests moved to "rescue" the flag, and a brief scuffle ensued between Lux and state senator Burnie Bauer. A faculty committee found that Lux had deliberately violated the IU policy forbidding demonstrations inside university buildings; furthermore, he encouraged students to do the same. The faculty recommended that Wolfson send Lux a formal letter of censure, which he did.

The second demonstration, entirely peaceful, occurred outdoors and did not violate any university policy. At the ground-breaking ceremonies for the addition to Northside Hall, held on May 6, 1970, a time of widespread demonstrations against President Richard Nixon's order to bomb Cambodia, the non-violent IUSB Coalition for Peace demonstrated against increased American bombing in and near Viet Nam. Despite rumors, no flags were destroyed, although symbolic dolls were buried in a newly-dug grave. One of the student leaders of the demonstration was Alice Wolfson, a daughter of the chancellor. Wolfson himself sent a letter on official IUSB letterhead stationery to President Nixon, expressing his "deep dismay at the extension of the war." Even more remarkably, Nixon replied some six weeks later.[11] The only violent act during this period of protest came a few weeks later, when two students armed with knives were spotted attempting to set fire to the auditorium. One of the students was a former president of the SDS. Both were soon arrested and later convicted of arson. Throughout this difficult period Wolfson modeled his consistent defense of academic freedom, as well as his concern for civility in argument and behavior, on the example of Herman B Wells.

This brief period of student activism in South Bend was a pale shadow of the student "riots" at the University of California in Berkeley, the University of Wisconsin in Madison, Columbia University in New York, or even IU's home campus in Bloomington. No one was injured at IUSB, no buildings were wrecked or burned, no dissident faculty were dismissed, and only the two arsonists were arrested. The one lasting symbol of the anti-war movement was the emergence of a real student newspaper from the turmoil of 1969. The *Student*, financed through student government, was challenged by three feisty news sheets, printed by barely legible mimeograph on the cheapest available paper. *Future* and *Recourse* soon vanished, but the *Preface* flourished. Its first issue appeared on March 27, 1969, and by the beginning of the fall semester in September it was IUSB's official student paper, now in tabloid format and professionally printed on good quality newsprint. The *Preface*, edited for its first few years by Margaret Grounds, was often critical of student government, as student newspapers usually are, but it was generally friendly toward faculty and administrators. Chancellor Wolfson promised the *Preface* his "total support." A student journalist quoted him as saying, in uncharacteristically informal language, that "A vital student newspaper is the best possible means there is to keep things percolating as they should within the university community."[12] Wolfson was not usually noted for his close association with individual students, but he did keep in close touch with editors and reporters for the *Preface*, gently nudging them in the directions of civility and good writing, while always defending them from external criticism. He was a true believer in freedom of the press, including student journalists accused of obscenity, rudeness, or a lack of patriotism.

Student requests for courses on black or Afro-American studies, as they were then known, also appeared in the late 1960s. Unlike so many other campuses in that turbulent era, IUSB students *asked for* such courses, and for the hiring of black faculty to teach them. There were no demands, no violent demonstrations, and no student take-over of the chancellor's office. During the 1968-69 academic year there was only one "Negro" faculty member at South Bend, and 36 in the entire university, a number which President Stahr believed to be "one of the highest in the nation, outside of predominately Negro institutions."[13] IUSB found it difficult to hire and retain African-American faculty, for a combination of financial and personal reasons, but their numbers increased slowly and without controversy. While Wolfson did not ever take a leading role in promoting faculty and student diversity, he adapted to the changing temper of the times and IUSB gradually hired and enrolled more women (although they were already a majority of students), more persons of color, and more faculty and then students from outside the United States. Gays and lesbians were few in number among faculty and staff, but they achieved promotion and tenure without particular difficulty.

Just a few months before Wolfson's retirement in 1987, he found himself involved in a final controversial defense of a surprising and unpopular cause—witchcraft. Dr. Gloria Kaufman, Chair of the Women's Studies program, invited a self-described witch named Z. Budapest to speak at IUSB. "Z," as she was called by both friends and opponents, referred to herself as the High Priestess of the Susan B. Anthony Coven Number One, and her remarks were emphatically anti-Christian. Beyond strong local criticism, IUSB was denounced by a conservative Catholic magazine in an article entitled "Witchcraft at Indiana University." In an eloquent response to critics outside the university, Wolfson wrote: "The dismal history of censorship should long ago have convinced reflective persons that it is far better to err on the side of what is permitted for discussion than on the side of what is forbidden."[14]

The Long Struggle to Build a Library

The Associates Investment Company was the richest and most prosperous corporation headquartered in South Bend after the close of Studebaker, but for IUSB it also represented a great obstacle. Located just across Greenlawn Avenue from the campus, its four buildings and spacious parking lots presented an impossible barrier to any westward expansion by IUSB. Limited on the north by busy Mishawaka Avenue and Potawatomi Park, and on the south by the St. Joseph River, IUSB's only hope for growth seemed to be eastward toward Ironwood Drive. Any such expansion would be both expensive and controversial through a residential neighborhood. Although legally the university could invoke eminent domain to acquire needed property, politically it could not dare to do so.

A glimmer of change appeared after 1968 when Associates was acquired by Gulf + Western, a large and rapidly expanding conglomerate eager to make use of its strong finances and large cash flow. Charles Bluhdorn, Gulf + Western's aggressive chairman, usually allowed the management of its subsidiaries wide discretion, and for a few years there was little change. By 1971 O. C. Carmichael, Jr., president of Associates, announced plans to build a new headquarters in downtown South Bend on a large site being cleared by the city's redevelopment department. Over the next few years there were extensive discussions between Associates and various university officers from Bloomington, including President John W. Ryan. All real estate matters were centrally managed, and the IUSB administration had no direct voice. By 1974 Carmichael and Ryan were in direct negotiations, and in January, 1975, Indiana University purchased the entire property from Associates First Capital Corporation for $6.8 million. Appraisers valued the property—13.5 acres, 270,000 square feet in four buildings, parking space for 900 vehicles, and 15 single-family houses on Hildreth and Esther streets—at $11.6 million, allowing Associates to take a large tax credit for its "gift" to the university. IUSB would eventually have ample space for its long-desired library, dozens of classrooms and offices, and also a fully equipped cafeteria.

The contract allowed Associates some three years to vacate the property, but in November, 1975, Gulf + Western startled everyone in South Bend with the announcement that the Associates offices would be moved as soon as possible to suburban Dallas. Only a few selected South Bend employees would be offered transfer to Texas. Associates further startled IUSB by handing over occupancy and full responsibility for the corporate offices and the cafeteria (now known as the Administration Building and the University Center) on October 15, 1976. Unfortunately there were no funds in the current budget for IUSB to cover even basic utility costs, because the transfer came more than a year before schedule. Embarrassed, IUSB could not make any use of its new property for many months.

Meanwhile, Gulf + Western closely examined the costs of moving the Associates data processing center to Dallas and decided that it would be more economical to keep it in South Bend. IUSB was placed in an impossible position: if it demanded occupancy, which was its right under the purchase contract, it would appear to cause the economically troubled community to lose 400 well-paid jobs. IUSB would simply have to find some other space for its library. What followed was a seemingly-endless argument over the precise terms by which Associates would rent the building from the university, with frequent extensions of its lease at gradually increasing payments. The rental payments provided some hope that there would eventually be sufficient money to build a library somewhere nearby, but at the time it was not even clear that the rent money would be used for the benefit of the South Bend campus. Legally the payments went to Indiana University. Associates First Capital did not hand over any part of the data processing center to IUSB until 2000, and yielded complete occupancy only in 2008, 33 years after it sold the building to the university. IUSB plans to begin a massive renovation of the building for classrooms, offices, and art studios in the fall of 2010.

The "library problem" began with the totally inadequate space in the original 1950s design of what became Northside Hall, a space no larger than the library of a contemporary suburban high school. Virtually every significant detail of the "IU Center" was well publicized at the time of construction, but neither the seating capacity nor the maximum number of volumes in the new library was ever mentioned. The expansion of degree programs after 1965 made the problem ever more acute, and the 1972 move to the Northside Hall addition was explicitly regarded as a temporary solution. With the Associates computer center settled in their leased building for as long as corporate execu-

*Formerly the Associates Computer Center, now the Education
and Arts Building*

tives wished to remain, the administration and faculty resumed their efforts to build a free-standing library. As most of them soon realized, a building designed from the beginning as a library would be far more suitable in the long run—but they had no idea that they would be forced to wait twelve more years.

Chancellor Wolfson, down deep always a professor of English, fully understood that the library was at the heart of any university. He had been consistently reluctant to engage in fund raising, but in order to build a library he developed an effective fund-raising program for IUSB and personally solicited donations. He was likewise reluctant to engage in any sort of political effort, but to build a library he found himself involved in a public dispute with the Indiana Commission for Higher Education, which vigorously opposed construction of a library for IUSB as an unnecessary extravagance. The faculty physical plant committee listed construction of a library as it first priority in the fall of 1965 and recommended a completion date of September 1968. Various faculty committees repeatedly listed a library building as IUSB's most pressing need year after year, and by 1971 the central IU administration tentatively allocated for South Bend $3.0 million for a library and $3.5 million for a student center. Precise locations were to be determined later. In 1972 Wolfson officially told the central administration that faculty, staff, and students at IUSB were frustrated by the persistent delay in library construction. Acquisition of the Associates property further delayed any decision about where to locate a library. Many persons in both South Bend and Bloomington viewed the red brick computing center as the most likely solution, although there were serious doubts about the building's suitability. In August, 1977, Associates notified IU that it would remain in the computing center at least until 1982. Wolfson learned this dreadful news from a report in the *South Bend Tribune*—neither IU nor Associates bothered to inform him directly. Late in 1981 the IU Trustees prepared to ask the state for $4.4 million to remodel the Associates data processing building for library use, but the Higher Education Commission opposed the request on the grounds that the Associates might remain indefinitely, and furthermore that IUSB did not really need expanded library facilities. In response, both the Academic Senate and the Student Government Association passed resolutions in February, 1982, in favor of building a new library. At the same time, IUSB finally began a serious effort to win community support for a new library. Indiana University, both centrally and through its South Bend campus, could not appear to push Associates and 400 well-paid jobs away from South Bend, but IUSB desperately needed to build a real library.

Almost everyone at IUSB, with the possible exception of the chancellor, believed that President Ryan and the IU central administration did not really care about building a library for South Bend, although there was a welcome increase in support from the Chamber of Commerce and from local legislators. In February, 1984, the IU Trustees extended the company's lease until 1994, with an option for a five-year extension. Clearly if IUSB were to have a library, it would require construction of a new building. In July, 1984, Wolfson optimistically told a *South Bend Tribune* reporter that the university was "exploring six or seven sites." He dreamed "The library should be ready by summer of 1987."[15] By the fall of 1984 the IUSB library had advanced on President Ryan's short list of four projects for state funding, and the corner of Greenlawn Avenue and Hildreth Street was identified as the site. This location required closing one block of Greenlawn and half a block of Hildreth, which led to a brief but heated controversy before city council gave its consent. A few years later the city agreed without dispute to close two additional blocks of Greenlawn, opening the way for the central mall which has become the well-landscaped core of the present campus. No one imagined that the state would appropriate the full cost of construction at a time of exceptionally tight budgets. In fact during 1983-1984 IUSB was forced to dismiss a small number of untenured faculty and a larger number of clerical and maintenance staff. Reluctantly, after twenty years in campus leadership, Lester Wolfson turned both institutionally and personally to asking businesses and individuals to give money to IUSB. Most of the detail work of fund-raising was done by John W. Sevier, formerly a professor of sociology and now special assistant to the chancellor. His particular responsibility was calling on area businesses.

IUSB's fund-raising effort was part of a university-wide campaign called the Campaign for Indiana, which was managed largely by the IU Foundation. Previous campaigns had almost completely neglected the regional campuses, but this time there was a strong local effort, chaired by Richard Rosenthal, president of the St. Joseph Bank in South Bend. The largest individual pledge was $300,000 from Franklin D. Schurz, chairman of the board of Schurz Communications, Inc, owner of the *South Bend Tribune* and WSBT television and radio. Wolfson apparently did not ask Schurz for his initial pledge in 1982, and at first the donation seemed intended to support "research aimed toward the economic development of the Michiana region." Gradually Wolfson brought the library into his correspondence with Schurz, but not until 1984 when it became clear that Associates would remain and a new library would be built. Even then he did not ask specifically that the money be designated for the library, although there was no doubt by the time that Schurz made the final payment on his pledge in 1986.[16] Wolfson had already formally asked President Ryan's permission to call the new building The Franklin D. Schurz Library. IUSB had to raise $2,000,000 in gifts to meet the anticipated cost of library construction, and the money did not come easily. In fact the full amount was not in hand, as usually required, before construction began. Associates First Capital, by the way, declined to make any contribution.

Wolfson's Legacy at IUSB

The formal ground-breaking ceremony for the Franklin D. Schurz Library was held on December 14, 1986, with the aged Schurz joining Chancellor Wolfson and President Ryan for the occasion. The ceremonial ground-breaking for a new building is a familiar event at American universities. Presidents, chancellors, and trustees take what might seem to those outside academia an exceptional delight in posing with polished shovels while pretending to dig small holes. But for those involved, this ground-breaking was indeed a memorable event, particularly for Chancellor Lester Wolfson, who had struggled through more than twenty years of academic, architectural, financial, and political frustration to win approval for the library he saw as the symbolic heart of the institution he had guided from a two-year program in a single building to a comprehensive regional campus offering more than two score associates, bachelors, and masters programs. Franklin D. Schurz, as publisher, editor, and community leader, could remember, even before Wolfson came to town, when the lights in the windows of Central High School showed that there was some semblance of public higher education in South Bend. For President John Ryan the memories were less exciting, for he was responsible for eight Indiana University campuses, but no one at IUSB ever doubted that his only true love was the beautiful and traditional campus in Bloomington.

Schurz probably did not yet know that Wolfson had told Ryan only two days earlier that he intended to retire as chancellor in September, 1987, almost a year before the mandatory retirement age for senior IU administrators. When and why Wolfson decided upon an early retirement remains a mystery. In August he had written to a foundation executive that he expected to preside at the opening of the library, in the fall of 1988, "during my twenty-fifth and final year as the chief officer of Indiana University at South Bend."[17] Ryan himself was a lame duck. He had announced six months earlier that he would retire in September, 1987, supposedly to work full time on the university's Campaign for Indiana.

Not until December 12 did Wolfson tell the Academic Senate of his intention to leave office almost twelve months before his mandatory retirement date. He made his announcement without fanfare, at the conclusion of his routine remarks, to the complete surprise of the IUSB faculty. This allowed ample time for the customary "search and screen" procedure by means of a large committee composed of faculty, staff, students, and community members. The final choice of the new chancellor would be made by President Ryan, in consultation with the incoming IU president, Thomas Ehrlich. Only in retrospect did the campus come to understand how unusual this smooth transition would be in the history of IUSB. Wolfson's predecessor, Jack Detzler, had been quietly removed in 1964. His successor, Daniel Cohen, would be removed in 1995 in the full glare of publicity and a succession of lawsuits. After two years of acting chancellor Les Lamon and one failed search, Kenneth Perrin began his troubled administration in 1997. He retired in 2005 and immediately moved away from South Bend, leaving a tangled budget, no office files at all, but twenty-eight staff positions filled on interim appointments. Chancellor Una Mae Reck soon remedied these administrative troubles, achieved full ten-year re-accreditation without reservations or qualifications, and returned IUSB to stability and sound finance in an era of diminishing state appropriations.

Franklin Schurz died in April, 1987, long before the Schurz Library was completed. The building was well under construction when Wolfson retired, and it opened its doors in January, 1989, at the beginning of the spring semester. Very appropriately, Chancellor Emeritus Lester Wolfson occupied an office on the second floor of the library. He had worked tirelessly for more than twenty years to achieve a proper library for IUSB. Nearing retirement, he wrote to the director of the Indiana Humanities Council: "You can always count on IUSB in its support of the humanities. Despite anything else, I think my proudest title is professor of English,"[18] and what better home for a retired English professor than the university library he had worked so hard to build.

Herman B Wells is without doubt the founder of Indiana University's system of regional campuses, a complex organization almost impossible to explain to visitors familiar with the better-known but quite different multi-campus systems in California, New York, and Wisconsin. Wells articulated a vision of two-year extension centers which would double as community cultural centers (hence their large auditoriums) and prevent the growth of an independent community college system which would diminish legislative appropriations for IU. In his memoirs, published in 1980, Wells looked back and observed that "the regional campuses have come of age and the university has become a multicampus institution in the truest sense." All in all, Wells concluded, "the [regional campus] system as it evolved offers to the state of Indiana the best possible program for the benefit of the students and all citizens of the state," providing "a widespread coverage of academic opportunities . . . with the least possible duplication and with the greatest efficiency."[19] Wolfson, always an admirer of Herman Wells, might not have agreed entirely, but throughout his years at IUSB he remained a loyal supporter of Indiana University as a statewide system, however frustrating its bureaucracy might become.

Even before the new university centers were built, students were seeking expanded course offerings, ideally leading to degree programs in all of Indiana's larger urban areas. This vital change was approved in principle for Indianapolis, Fort Wayne, Gary, and South Bend in 1965, presenting Les Wolfson with a remarkable challenge—the opportunity to shape an underfunded branch campus into a not-quite-autonomous small university. Before 1965, all important decisions for the South Bend campus were made in the president's office in Bloomington or by the General Assembly in Indianapolis. From now on, the academic leadership in South Bend, with whatever local political support it could find, would be able to shape a distinctive curriculum, to define its own admissions policy, and to recruit a faculty to carry out its plans. Of course there would be endless struggles with the central administration in Bloomington and for a time the micro-management of the vice-president for Regional Campus Administration in Indianapolis, as well as the often heavy hand of the Indiana Commission on Higher Education, *but after 1965 the initiative would always come from IUSB*. Lester Wolfson was never the only one at IUSB with ideas for new programs, new policies, and new buildings, but only he was in a position to say *yea* or *nay* about which proposals would go forward from the campus to whatever higher powers controlled the campus budget and the approval or denial of new degree programs. IUSB's emphasis on fine arts, music, and theater, its emphasis on student writing, its rigorous requirements for tenure and promotion, all reflect the mind, the personality, and the eloquence of Lester Wolfson.

Endnotes

[1] See, for example, Arthur W. Chickering, *The Modern American College* (San Francisco: Jossey-Bass, 1981). Neither "regional campus" nor "branch campus" is recognized in the standard classification scheme, *Classification of Institutions of Higher Education* (Princeton, N.J.: Carnegie Foundation for the Advancement of Teaching, 1987), 7-8. *American Universities and Colleges*, 18th edition (Westport, Conn.: Praeger, 2008), I, xiv-xv, lists "branch campus" among its defined terms, but not "regional campus." The Southern Branch started with a two-year transfer program but began offering a four-year degree program in 1922 and graduate degrees in 1933. For a very brief history, see *American Universities and Colleges*, I, 157.

[2] "Inaugural Address of Herman B Wells," December 1, 1938, in Thomas D. Clark, *Indiana University: Midwestern Pioneer*, Vol. IV, *Historical Documents Since 1816* (Bloomington: Indiana University, 1977), 376-84. Quotation at 379. A brief account of the expansion of IU's extension centers into regional campuses may be found in Thomas D. Clark, *Indiana University: Midwestern Pioneer, Vol. III, Years of Fulfillment* (Bloomington: Indiana University Press, 1977), 614-18. The importance of the regional campuses, as viewed from Bloomington, is shown with painful clarity by these four pages in a volume which covers the entire university from 1938 until 1968 in 648 pages of text. A more detailed account appears in Herman B Wells, *Being Lucky: Reminiscences and Reflections* (Bloomington (Indiana University Press), 118-19, 210-11, 230-35. Students of IU trivia and learned copy editors know that President Wells had only the letter B for his middle name. Because it is not abbreviated, it does not require a period.

[3] Herman B Wells to M. M. Chambers [University of Michigan], December 29, 1960; copies sent to center directors March 30 1961, Lester M. Wolfson Papers, IUSB Archives, Unnumbered Box "Bloomington Correspondence, 1957-1972."

[4] Wells, *Being Lucky*, 103; P. J. Furlong, interview with Wells, November 12, 1981; Dedication program for Indiana University Center, South Bend-Mishawaka Campus, March 25, 1962, copy in Wolfson Papers, Box 59, Folder 14. The formal proposal for the "university centers," not yet called regional campuses, was made in 1955 by Hugh W. Norman, Dean of Adult Education and Public Services. See Clark, *Historical Documents*, 690-91.

[5] Stahr's "Statement to the Board of Trustees," April 19, 1968, is in Clark, *Historical Documents*, 749-55. It was in this "Statement" that Stahr proposed renaming the regional campuses, thus creating "IUSB."

[6] Wolfson to Ryan, November 27, 1968, Wolfson Papers, Unnumbered Box, "President John Ryan, 1970-1986."

[7] Demaree to "Distribution Indicated," December 14, 1973, Wolfson Papers, Box 80, Folder "Arts [Music]."

[8] Statement by Dean Elizabeth K. Grossman, June 12, 1986, Wolfson Papers, Box 63, Folder 1.

[9] Kevin Upton to Wolfson, December 1, 1971; Wolfson to Walt P. Risler, December 3, 1971; Wolfson to Upton, January 13, 1972; Wolfson to Ryan, October 11, 1985; IUSB Press Release, March 13, 1986; all in Wolfson Papers, Box 7, Folder 4, Box "Ad. Com., 1985-87," Box 4, Folder 16.

[10] Wolfson to Edgar G. Williams, July 24, 1986, Wolfson Papers, Box 28, Folder "President Ryan."

[11] *Preface*, May 14, 1970; Wolfson to Richard M. Nixon, May 5, 1970; Nixon to Wolfson, June 24, 1970, Wolfson Papers, Box 10, Folder 3.

[12] *Preface*, March 27, September 10, 1969.

[13] Stahr's speech to the Statewide Conference on the Negro in Higher Education, May 17, 1968, in Clark, *Historical Documents*, 759-73. Quotation at 769. This lengthy and very detailed report was the first occasion when a president of Indiana University formally addressed racial issues on its campuses.

[14] E. Michael Jones, "Witchcraft at Indiana University," *Fidelity* (May 1987); Wolfson to Kevin G. Long [Director of Public Affairs for the Catholic League for Religious and Civil Rights], March 30, 1987, Wolfson papers, Box 15, Folder 18.

[15] Carla Hoffman, "Wolfson Discusses Past and Future Goals for IUSB," *South Bend Tribune*, July 15, 1984.

[16] Wolfson to Franklin D. Schurz, December 16, 1983, January 3, August 22, September 18, December 17, 1984, February 7, 1986, all letters in Wolfson Papers, Box 14, Folder 11.

[17] Wolfson to Ryan, December 12, 1986, Wolfson Papers, Box 26, Folder "President Ryan," copy in Box 58, Folder 6; Wolfson to H. G. Mass, August 21, 1986, Wolfson Papers, Box 10, Folder 13.

[18] Wolfson to Kenneth L. Gladish, April 2, 1985, Wolfson Papers, Box 8, Folder 2.

[19] Wells, *Being Lucky*, 118-19, 235.

"I fall upon the thorns of life! I bleed!"

A playful administrative team poses for the Analecta *literary magazine:*
Walt Risler, Lester Wolfson, and Albert Beutler.

An IUSB Chronology

1922   First IU extension classes in South Bend

1933   Start of regular extension classes at Central High School

1940   First resident administrator, Lynton K. Caldwell

1941   First permanent full-time faculty member, Dr. Ernest Gerkin

1944   Dr. Donald F. Carmony named director

1950   Jack L. Detzler named director

1961   IU Center opens on riverside campus, later named Northside Hall

1962   Extension Center renamed South Bend-Mishawaka Campus

1964   Dr. Lester M. Wolfson named director and dean

1965   Four-year degree programs authorized

1967   First Commencement–31 degrees awarded

1968   IUSB gets its nickname–officially Indiana University at South Bend

1970   Anti-war demonstrations on campus; first master's degrees conferred

1971   Enrollment exceeds 5,000

1972   Northside Hall West Addition opens

1975   Purchase of Associates Investment Co. buildings greatly enlarges campus

1986   Groundbreaking for Schurz Library

1987   Chancellor Wolfson retires, succeeded by H. Daniel Cohen

1989   Schurz Library opens

Changing Names

Indiana University began offering credit classes in South Bend's downtown Central High School in 1933 under the name **Extension Center**. Accurate enough for the 1930s, "the Extension" became in time a despised and misleading label, which persisted in popular usage until the early 1970s. The official name from the mid-1930s was **South Bend-Mishawaka Center**. From 1962 the various IU extension centers were officially described as **regional campuses**. When classes moved to the riverside site in 1961, the new building was called **Indiana University Center**, and the following year its setting became the **South Bend-Mishawaka Campus**. The confusion continued when the IU Trustees renamed all of the regional campuses in the spring of 1968. **Indiana University—South Bend** was the official name for less than a month, becoming **Indiana University at South Bend** in early July of 1968. **IUSB** immediately became the informal name used by students, faculty, and even senior university administrators. **Indiana University South Bend** has been the official name since September, 1992. In more recent years the campus has also been referred to as **IU South Bend**.

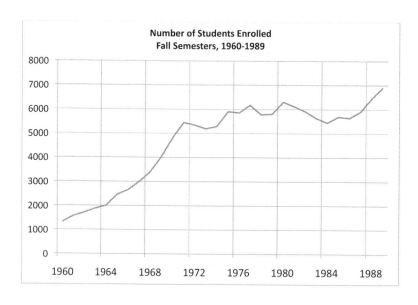

Campus Buildings During the Wolfson Years

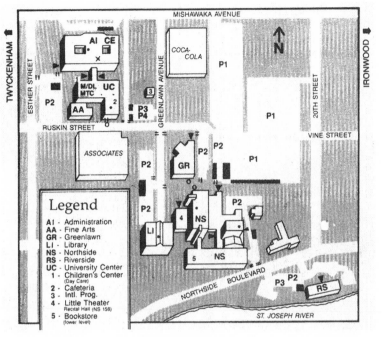

Campus map, 1989

Lester Wolfson with Herman B Wells, President of IU from 1938-62, and Chancellor from 1962-2000

"What's it all about, Alfie?"
Tom R. Vander Ven

Les Wolfson didn't allude to popular culture very often, but his frequent question, borrowed from the movie and song, became a motif with a number of his colleagues over the course of his twenty-three years as chancellor of Indiana University South Bend. The movie *Alfie* asked the question in 1966, and the chancellor was still asking us decades later. His tone was typically one of playful bemusement, at times feigned. Abstracted from the erotic compulsion of the movie's title character and from the song's plaintive belief in love (without which we merely exist), his question seemed to be both ritual and code. And at the end of a brief letter in March of 2009, citing a close friend who had recently chided his agnosticism while affirming that, for him, "conversion to Roman Catholicism had made all the difference," Wolfson concludes, "What's it all about, Alfie?" This had become his way to embrace American society in the language of its popular culture, while asking it to ponder the many possible answers to a profound and abiding existential question.

Wolfson had boundless recall, and he found his own freely associative mind irresistible. Once he had begun a story, only a tornado warning or a fire alarm could stop him. But he was never dogged or facile. He loved life and its stories, from his own experience and from literature, and he often compounded the two. He would not only quote from his own speeches in a conversation; he would return to his office and send someone the full text. He didn't want the conversation to end—which led to long lunches, extra drinks, followed by an envelope in the campus mail. "What's it all about?" was a prelude to lunch and to conversation on everything from current campus issues of curriculum and budget to tectonic questions of self-knowledge and cosmic design. Wolfson would not have said somberly, "Let us contemplate the mysteries," but that is what he liked to do, even preferred to do, no matter how dreary the leaden Novembers of South Bend, no matter how labored or tendentious the debate had become at a monthly meeting of the faculty's Academic Senate, which he once called a "training ground for stand-up comedians."

Linda Fritschner, Sociology, who came to IUSB in 1980, recalls when Les Wolfson "would invite junior faculty to lunch." His interest in and informal contact with his colleagues might appear to academics in 2010 as a quaint expression of an era of innocence—of an English professor-cum-chancellor, presiding over a small, one-building campus. There were 2,000 students in his first year, 1964, doubling to 4,000 in his first five years, and growing from 26 faculty to 106 in that same time. In the '60s, everyone at IUSB knew everyone else, or at least knew stories about everyone else. While the logistics of a little campus enabled the comforts and misdemeanors of a single, communal coffee lounge, Les Wolfson did bring to South Bend an idea of the university as an academic and cultural community, not only in formal research and in pedagogy, but also in collegial, even familial conversation.

His personal engagement with faculty was expressive both of his personality and of his vision of the university. He interviewed virtually all on-campus finalists for academic appointments, and he asked substantive questions that showed he had read our resumes, and, of course, with his remarkable memory, he could allude to our careers and our research and, as in my interview, quote at length from the poetry of Robert Frost. His Ph.D. was in English, but his wide reading and his love of art and music infused his voice with countless allusions to and citations from intellectual and cultural history. Wolfson's collegial enthusiasm played a critical role in his leadership of an emergent regional campus. The faculty he recommended for appointment helped define the kind of campus he envisioned for north-central Indiana.

Informal conversations with faculty, annual university addresses, both to the faculty at the autumn senate meetings and to the graduates at May commencements, periodic papers delivered at diverse events, play across the years from 1964 to 1987 as scenes from a marriage of contemplative, energetic, and even, at times, combative minds. Those years forged a visible and coherent regional campus identity where, since the 1930s, there had been only part-time, evening classes, taught by part-time faculty, meeting in what Wolfson would call the "sardine-can intimacy at Central High School."

I do not write this to belittle beginnings; during the months soon after Keats's birth, he was a necessary baby. Rather, I make this reference in an attempt to measure those transformative, institutional years which Lester Wolfson's presence and vision so greatly guided.

A Center of Consciousness

He was someone whose mind and voice shaped large social circumferences, as well as the rooms he entered.

Like our nation's constitution, "a machine that would go of itself," an academic institution turns fitfully and inexorably by semesters and syllabi, by departmental meetings and retreats, and by enrollments and budget appropriations, whether its chief administrative officer is from time to time asleep or delusional. How does one offer a clear, causal proof that one man with a Ph.D. in English Literature and one or another administrative titles has made all the difference over nearly a quarter century? One does not. And yet the memories of his colleagues and the mass of archived texts of his speeches and writings affirm his benevolent advocacy of art, intellect, academic integrity, and social responsibility at Indiana University's campus on the St. Joseph River. Those memories are not nostalgic hymns of praise; rather, they tell the story of coequal conversations between the chancellor and faculty.

Sandra Winicur, Biology, tells of pointing out to Wolfson a negative side-effect on biology classes of an administrative decision to move forward the mid-semester spring break: "We came to school while the frogs were still hibernating. I tried to explain, but didn't get anywhere, with literary references to frogs passing back and forth."

Conversations with Les Wolfson were not always dialogues. Don Sloan, English, once described the chancellor as a "center of consciousness"; he was someone whose mind and voice shaped large social circumferences, as well as the rooms he entered, a jar placed in Tennessee. Part of his conversational power lay in his embracing mental processes. Everything reminded him of something else. And part of the energy appeared to be a compulsion to do all the talking. At one conversation over lunch, Les grew monologic, until I finally asked, "Am I going to be allowed to talk?" He laughed, said, "No," and resumed talking.

During IUSB's night-school phase in the 1930s, '40s, and '50s, as an extension center for the Bloomington campus, Les Wolfson finished high school in Grand Rapids, Michigan, then matriculated to the University of Michigan in 1941, and, finally, while holding instructorships at Wayne University in Detroit (now Wayne State) and at the University of Houston, completed a Ph.D. at Ann Arbor in 1954, at the age of 30.

In 1962, when the South Bend-Mishawaka campus opened North-side Hall on its present river campus of twelve buildings, Wolfson was an assistant professor of English at IU-Northwest in Gary, another of the small, growing campuses in the Indiana system. Except for a visiting appointment of one year, 1958-59, at the University of California, Santa Barbara, he had been a faculty member in Indiana University's constellation of campuses since 1955, eight of the nine years before he came to South Bend as chief administrative officer. In his last two years at the Gary campus, he had served as an academic counselor, then as chair of English.

The appointment of Les Wolfson as director in 1964 proved to be a fortuitous, harmonic convergence of a barely visible, unhistoried, evening campus with a forty-year-old professor of English embarking on a career in university administration. South Bend, in north-central Indiana, had been a city of manufacturing since the mid-19th century—most notably, the Studebaker Corporation (wagons and automobiles, 1852-1963) and the Oliver Corporation (plows and other farm equipment, 1850s-1976)—as well as the site of the University of Notre Dame since 1842. Grand Rapids, in western Michigan, where Wolfson grew up, had a similar history—a city of automotive parts and furniture manufacturing, and the site since 1876 of Calvin College.

Unlike these two well-established private schools, the new South Bend-Mishawaka campus of Indiana University had no degree programs, no alumni, no regional identity, and, in the sports-shadow of Notre Dame football, almost no prospect of gaining the region's attention through an athletics program. But the path to recognition through sports programs did not interest Wolfson; in 1964 he said that he had "no sympathy with the disproportionate attention given to intercollegiate athletics." He was a closet Detroit Tigers baseball fan, and he had an occasional tepid interest in the Wolverines of his alma mater, but he did not during his career promote athletics at IUSB. The university has avoided what Mike Washburn, Philosophy, calls the "false tribal consciousness" of high visibility sports. Though the school has had some very good NAIA men's and women's varsity basketball teams, IUSB alumni may never see their teams on television or tailgate before a game; they will have to content themselves with reminiscences of a life of the mind. What Wolfson brought to the little campus, which area residents continued to call "the extension" years after it developed and administered its own degree programs with campus-specific requirements, was his abiding love of the academy—of the humanities, the sciences, professional programs, art, music, and theatre. And to create such a campus in South Bend was why he came. According to Eileen Bender, English, Wolfson's vision distinguished IUSB from the other regional campuses: "This is the only regional campus that created a liberal arts core."

His speeches were often a one-man colloquium of the great thinkers and writers living in his mind, with whom he conferred as he spoke. Harold Zisla, Fine Arts, said that Wolfson's speeches were "done in his head, and he would just sit down and write 'em down. But he couldn't tie his shoes so Velcro was a godsend."

That capability he indeed confirmed in the way he conversed—at length, coherently, and with instant and precise recitation of a wide range of texts. There were throughout his informal and formal remarks apt digressions, allusions-on-the-fly, and often quotations from his own speeches and writings.

In 1970, in what he referred to as his "seventh September," he addressed the faculty on "the urgency of the current problems in university institutional life." He embraced that sense of urgency with allusions and references to the elegiac ballad, "September Song," Greek mythology's Pelion upon Ossa, Socrates, Adam's naming of the hippopotamus (by inference), Dante's Tiresias, *Romeo and Juliet*, Henry James's short story, "The Beast in the Jungle," Joseph Heller's *Catch-22*, and Saul Bellow's *Mr. Sammler's Planet*. Wolfson's confidence in the relevance of cultural history to the immediate, tumultuous state of political and intellectual conflict in America and its universities stood undaunted. He would swaddle the bleating moment in the cloth of human history. He believed in literature's cloak. He cited Tybalt as a figure looking for a fight. He invoked Tiresias as a caution against prophetic vision. And he offered Sammler as an affirmation of those things that ought not to be changed for the sake of change. He averred the Wolfsonian discourse of the middle ground: that we should neither claim to know too much nor seek too confidently to alter what we have.

Uncivility: A Beast in the Jungle

During a few days in May, of protests and rioting at Kent State University,
Ohio, the unwarranted shooting of students by national guardsmen had been
followed by protests and school closings at
hundreds of colleges and universities across America.

After noting the promising and rapid growth of the campus—in enrollment, credit hours, faculty, and budget (five times what it had been in his first year)—his 1970 remarks turned to "a beast that lurks in the jungle," one "far more gross" than the beast of Henry James's short story. He described an uncivil, predatory beast which he believed now threatened reasonable discourse and the tolerance of differing views in the forum of university life. The academy suffered a climate of "fundamental disrespect for, and suspicion of, the informed heart and mind," which he believed it is the academy's duty to nurture.

While some of IUSB's students and faculty had become active in organizing protests against the Vietnam War, events on campus were small, orderly, and not reported nationally by media, where attention focused on larger, more dramatic venues such as Columbia and Berkeley. And yet some IUSB faculty felt that campus events were being appropriated as ideological anti-war forums and parades, with students carrying baby dolls with missing limbs, smeared with red. Four months before, in May, during a few days of protests and rioting at Kent State University, Ohio, the unwarranted shooting of students by national guardsmen had been followed by protests and school closings at hundreds of colleges and universities across America.

Had the middle ground been lost? IUSB, like the nation at large, had become polarized between those who affirmed the American foreign policy of military intervention and those who had lost faith in the democratic, political process. Some faculty believed that it was no longer possible to take a middle ground—to voice reasoned opposition to the Vietnam War but not to engage in angry street protests. Yet Wolfson concluded his September talk by affirming the need "to get matters back in hand," and "to be modest about what we can do institutionally to solve social problems directly."

Few years in IUSB's history were so controversial, though Wolfson maintained a calm confidence, trying always to moderate a volatile and unreasonable climate of discourse. He administered the predicament of exploring ideas in a disinterested spirit, of refining artistic sensibility in theatre and music, and of illuminating decent and reasonable moral choices, while serving a society that had become confrontational and at times violently political.

When the 1960s had begun, Wolfson, like most Americans, could not have foreseen the upheaval ahead. The necessary struggle to win full civil rights for all Americans destabilized entrenched social custom and civil law. Then the eruptive debate over the purpose and execution of the war in Vietnam further polarized the country. Wolfson's appointment at South Bend came in 1964, the same year as the Gulf of Tonkin incident, the beginning of the country's tragic envelopment in a war of attrition half a planet away.

Given human history, neither could Wolfson have expected higher education to flower in fields of social tranquility. He knew that humanity and its institutions were problematic. The work of a chancellor was problematic. He had addressed an honors convocation at Bethel College in 1967, invoking for the students the admirable, delusional figure of Don Quixote as his mad emblem of human nature: ". . . you should keep unwavering faith in your convictions—religious, cultural and intellectual, even when the whole force of modernity or expedience whispers or shouts that you are wrong." Here was Lester

Wolfson, raised a Jew in Protestant Grand Rapids, celebrating a mad, fictional Spanish Catholic, and urging the students at a conservative, evangelical Christian college in Indiana to "advance over our desert places within, our dark inarticulateness," on "a journey to the light." Wolfson affirmed that the true god, a very generalized, non-denominational god, is Love. Then he ended his part in the honoring event by reading a Richard Wilbur poem, difficult in its diction and syntax: "We fray into the future, rarely wrought / Save in the tapestries of afterthought," and risky in its celebration of the "perfection in the death of ferns / Which laid their fragile cheeks against the stone / A million years." Buried in this text of fossil ferns was a scientific assumption about a very ancient earth. To this audience, Wolfson, warmly charming, as he always would be, may himself have seemed, if not Quixotic, somewhat abstracted, other-dimensional, and even wrong about creation.

His speech on Cervantes applied the vision he articulated in an essay as a junior at the University of Michigan in 1943; a stern and alarmed undergraduate Wolfson wrote about the problem of ideals in American society. In that A+ hand-written essay for English 71, he declared the failure of the home, the church, the school, and their leaders, in "the inculcation of moral and intellectual virtues." He called his generation "mental cripples and moral dwarfs." He had "little hope that our children will be any better . . . . our age is one which respects nothing . . . . we have lost our humanity." Wolfson, were he to read now his own prose of sixty-six years ago, would no doubt readily acknowledge the irony of denouncing a failed society that had produced him, as well as the men and women who fought and died in World War II, memorialized darkly in Norman Mailer's novel, *The Naked and the Dead* (1948), and lovingly in Tom Brokaw's narrative, *The Greatest Generation* (1998). As an undergraduate, he believed that the liberal arts of St. John's College, Annapolis, held the one hope for the recovery of a declining society through study of the great writings of civilization in their primary sources.

A decade later, he voiced grave concern that higher education had lost it awareness of and relevance to the "great world outside our classrooms and libraries." Teaching at the University of Houston in 1954, he wrote of "the terrifying power of the hydrogen bomb, coupled with the brutish irrationalities which underestimate its danger." He urged that each graduate student, in choosing an area of research, must

> scrutinize carefully his present activities in search of a morally valid justification for them. . . . That there is value in the disinterested search for what is true, none but the most benighted will deny. But the type of busy-work research which results in such papers as 'Beowulf's Armlock on Grendel in the Light of Modern Wrestling Technique' should make any young American scholar blush for his profession.

Endeavor After Man's Perfection

He voiced as chancellor the compelling design he found in all things, and which he sought to express in the growth of the IUSB campus.

By the time Wolfson came to South Bend in 1964, the gloomy elegy of the 1943 essay and the bleak jeremiad of the 1954 article had given way to inspirational advocacy, though not without alarm bells. The scholarly, high cultural cast of his vision and the language of that vision affirmed the critical role of higher education. Even a small, new Midwestern regional campus, he averred, could commit itself to what Matthew Arnold called "the disinterested endeavour after man's perfection" (*Culture and Anarchy*). Reason, knowledge, and goodness were kindred values. His affirmation in the Houston article of "the Socratic doctrine that the good man is usually the man who knows, and who knows what he does not know" echoed in later speeches to IUSB's faculty.

He was himself a generous, decent, knowing man, with a humble awareness of the limits of his knowing—an exemplary union of qualities that did not fail. Which is not to write worshipfully that he was never wrong, nor that he always knew when he was wrong. But he served the university and its community with a husbandman's earnest dissemination of ideas and allusions to the great and not-so-great thinkers and artists who had shaped his vision. Chaucer. Shakespeare. Cervantes. Out of the 19th century, he cited Keats, Wordsworth,

Arnold, and Cardinal Newman, and from the 20th century, his references ranged across Frost, Millay, Wilbur, Malamud, Bellow, and Max Shulman, whose popular satires included the novel, *I Was a Teenage Dwarf.*

On many occasions, he celebrated his high school English teacher, Olga Perschbacher, who introduced him to Wordsworth, diverting him from the study of law to English. In 1993, speaking at Evangel Heights United Methodist Church in South Bend, he recalled how she had introduced him to Wordsworth's "Ode: Intimations of Immortality": ". . . at birth we come 'trailing clouds of glory from God who is our home.'" He told that audience how, nearly forty years before, he had ended his doctoral dissertation on Keats with the affirmation that Keats's odes "are evidence of that great Love which binds all things each to each."

Some of us in academia find few occasions and even less courage to speak outside of the classroom of our special expertise; we may even be quietly embarrassed by the Grendelian armlocks of our own specialized research, but Les Wolfson imagined all audiences as willing listeners to the truths about humanity that he found affirmed by music and literature. He voiced as chancellor the compelling design he found in all things, and which he sought to express in the growth of the IUSB campus.

In a sense, his career as a leader in higher education articulated Keats's binding "great Love," a flowering of sorts, like Wordsworth's daffodils, or Olga Perschbacher, caring for "the roses that have been in the refrigerator since the day before . . . arranging them in bouquets throughout the house. . . . with seven vases organized on a structure which holds them high and in a graceful design." In his 1983 address to the faculty, "Like Grim Death," Wolfson recalled another great influence on his literary life. His undergraduate honors tutor, H. T. (Hereward Thimbleby) Price, taught him about the comprehensive, organic design in Shakespeare's plays, but "fell into bushes when he leaned forward to smell the flowers." Wolfson's comic spirit rose up in that evocation of a professor with a Dickensian name, who "by all the text-book criteria of what makes for effective teaching . . . would have to be judged a failure." Here Wolfson captures the comedy of the academy, of professors exclaiming on the tragedy of Othello or the savagery of Gettysburg or the evocation of Alpine horns in Brahms's 1st Symphony, wearing jackets elbowed in chalk dust or lecturing, as one math colleague did, wearing one brown shoe and one black.

His texts were woven of innumerable threads of literary history and contemporary, popular culture. While Wolfson would cite in a single paragraph four major literary figures—Shakespeare, Dryden, Pope, and Arnold, he also alluded to "Mammy Yokum trances" (of the "Lil' Abner" cartoon, 1934-1977) and to the "TV Tarzan in the beer ad." One fall, he asked, "Why, during the first week of classes, is the voice of the air hammer heard in our land?" Audible at times in Wolfson's prose is the Chicago-style intellect of the busy streets of Bellow's *Henderson the Rain King*: I love the old bitch [reality] just the way she is and I like to think I am always prepared for even the very worst she has to show me. I am a true adorer of life, and if I can't reach as high as the face of it, I plant my kiss somewhere lower down. Wolfson knew that IUSB's campus was not a Michelangelo-designed Campidoglio. It was a commuter campus in what had always been a manufacturing town.

And of the Curveship Lend a Myth

He told me that the campus would one day expand to the land across the river with the building of a campus footbridge—a symbol of the university as a cultural span.

Yet he wanted the best possible education for the students of the region. For this campus he sought an academic culture beyond the profession-centered degree programs in marketing, finance, and accounting, of teacher training, and of medical and dental technology, which other minds in Indiana's higher education planning sought as restrictive and practical regional supplements to the broader intellectual research and artistic expression of the state's public flagship institutions in Bloomington and West Lafayette. In addition to professional and technical programs for the region, Wolfson's vision engendered for South Bend a strong liberal arts curriculum, with degree programs in literature, philosophy, history, foreign languages, behavioral and physical sciences, mathematics, fine arts, theatre, and music. (During his years, computer science was still a nascent discipline.) Faculty came

Bernadine Oliphent coaches a voice student

to IUSB from some of the best doctoral programs, such as Princeton, North Carolina, Virginia, the University of Chicago, Indiana, the University of Michigan, Wisconsin, Iowa, Stanford, California Riverside, the University of London, and Oxford. And many of us were persuaded of the potential of the campus by the presence of Les Wolfson—glimpsed in a recruitment interview in his office in Northside Hall, overlooking the river and what was then the Playland golf course and the concrete ruins of the auto racetrack bleachers. In 1966, at my recruitment interview, he told me that the campus would one day expand to the land across the river with the building of a campus footbridge—a symbol of the university as a cultural span. I believed him. And IUSB's footbridge came to pass, not unlike Hart Crane's poetic bridge:

> Under thy shadow by the piers I waited;
> Only in darkness is thy shadow clear.
> The City's fiery parcels all undone,
> Already snow submerges an iron year . . .
>
> O Sleepless as the river under thee,
> Vaulting the sea, the prairies' dreaming sod,

Footbridge over the St. Joseph River, Schurz Library in the background

Unto us lowliest sometime sweep, descend
And of the curveship lend a myth to God.

Crane's hymn to the Brooklyn Bridge is all grandeur of darkness, light, and cultural myth, none of which anyone attributes straight-faced and metaphorically to the red IUSB footbridge that now joins the working campus to student apartments and parking lots.

But we learned slowly of the impeded dream of the bridge through periods of oil crisis, economic recession, state budget deficit, land acquisition negotiation, and river management by the Army Corps of Engineers. I would not cross that promised footbridge until the next century—a few years after I retired and a full two decades after Wolfson retired.

The chancellor's own career path had led over a bridge from the usual scholarly specialization in an English department toward the administrative design of a traditional campus, integral with its community and the world at large. He was a vigorous advocate of majors in music, theatre, and fine arts. He established the very fine Chester String Quartet, and he wrote program notes for Joseph Green's production of *Romeo and Juliet* (1965) and for *The Merchant of Venice* (1985), one of the many artfully-costumed productions of Warren

IU South Bend theater productions: U.L.: Mask from Oedipus Rex; *U.R.: Tiny Tim, from* A Christmas Carol, *12/22/73; L.L.: scene from* Hedda Gabler, *4/21/76*

Pepperdine over his long career. The annual Wolfson Literary Awards (so named during his tenure), conducted by the Department of English, were funded by an endowment in his name, and for many years he would remember in remarks at that event the benefactors, Richard and Margaret McCormack (she was an alumna of his early years at IUSB).

The Department of Philosophy, with its faculty's excellent credentials, offered an undergraduate degree in philosophy and contributed

Chester String Quartet, L-R: Ronald Gorevic, Thomas Rosenberg, Susan Frier, Fritz Gearhart

to a luxury of humanities that few such small schools could sustain. For all his executive responsibilities, Wolfson himself attended the annual Philosophy Day lecture and discussion. His genial wit and reflective spirit at such events as an advocate of ideas and the arts gave to the campus some of the "personal grace" that he believed had been lost in American life. In 1967, he said, "The main thing I have learned—or re-learned—from the Miss Lonelyhearts aspects of my present job, is that the root problems of American education. . . are not so much intellectual or even moral, but are, rather, aesthetic. . . . such Norman Rockwell sentimentalities; so little of the Wordsworthian power to imagine that which we know; so many remnants of Puritan constriction."

Despite Wolfson's protests about the state of American education, his tone always sought to lift up IUSB's sense of its mission. He perceived the role of rhetoric and public speaking as a synthesizing act; his speeches themselves were communal acts of exhortation and celebration. In 1954, in an address to teachers of speech, published later in the *Southern Communication Journal,* he said: ". . . if we resolve that all our studies be grounded in an unquenchable desire to make 'reason and the will of God prevail,' speech may yet be a prime means to save us

Lester Wolfson and Walton Collins receive awards of appreciation from the IU South Bend Women's Club, 1975

from ever-onrushing night. More than that, it will make what is saved well worth the saving." His call for resolve and unquenchable desire sought a balance between the exercise of human reason in social institutions and the cosmic dominion of divine will. (The latter he would invoke explicitly only a few times in his career, though he may well have assumed providential power as the abiding force behind human endeavor, of which more later in this discussion.)

Wolfson did not use the term "reason" to objectify human thinking, to "elevate intellect and deny the passions." Speaking in New York in 1960 at a convention of the Speech Association of the Eastern States, he warned that science's

> theoretical and practical triumphs have served to devalue, in subtle ways, literature, the arts, and the immediacies of human communication in the personal interchange of formal and informal speaking . . . . Traditional philosophic and scientific views in various ways treat men as things rather than

as persons who through their autonomous choices determine what and that they shall be.

He believed in higher education as a place that should make such autonomous choices possible. In its most grand spirit, higher education was the liberating exploration of the history of great minds and writers; in the daily flux of hallways and classrooms, as Assistant to the Chancellor (1969-1983) and close friend, Walt Collins, says, Wolfson wanted us to live our learning as "two men on a log having a conversation." Collins, who came to IUSB from a career as an editor at *The South Bend Tribune,* had a keen ear for the use and misuse of language and shared with Wolfson "moments of mild exasperation with the

L-R: Tom Vander Ven, Les Lamon, Brenda Knowles, Harold Zisla, John Russo, Wayne Bartholomew, Earl Savage, all-university distinguished teaching award winners

jargon of academic disciplines." Collins recalls a meeting with Director of Continuing Education Jim Ryan, at which Ryan closed with the observation that the discussion had managed to establish the horizontal axis of a problem, and what remained was to identify the vertical axis. After that meeting, Collins suggested to Ryan that they grasp the horizontal axis firmly and rotate it ninety degrees. Like Wolfson, Collins was a man of amused patience, as was another influential figure in the Wolfson administration, Walt Risler, Sociology, and for many years during the Wolfson tenure, Dean of Faculties (before title inflation). In the days when smoke was legal in public places, Risler kept a cigarette lit much of the time, talking through a cloud. None of these men ever showed anger in debate, but the rest of us around the table had better be alert. Risler would offer an insight, pause, and ask, "Get it? Get it?" Or he might say offhandedly, "A chimpanzee in a sport coat could figure that out."

By the later years of Wolfson's tenure as chancellor, IUSB's commitment to leadership in education produced a higher percentage of

Harold Zisla

all-university teaching awards than at any other IU campus. Wolfson valued that achievement; he attended the honors convocations in Bloomington at which those awards were conferred. John Russo, Computer Sciences, remembers the awards as a celebration of IUSB's high standards: "Les took winners out to dinner. The waiter put the napkin in my lap, and I knew it was serious then." It would be difficult to overstate the degree of comfortable access to the administration that the faculty had during the Wolfson years.

Still, all administrators' visions have peripheries, and Wolfson's generous sense of the university as an "active cloister" appears to have had its margins. When women faculty met with Wolfson to discuss the status of women at IUSB, arguing for more vigorous recruitment, Sandra Winicur recalls Wolfson saying that "the History department had nine males, no females, and, if they were comfortable with that, that was all right. He was telling this to the Women's Caucus. . . . He saw IU as a community of scholars. And that didn't include women." Wolfson was never aggressive in advocating cultural change within the institution. He neither demanded it, nor did he insistently resist it.

While Wolfson viewed across the curveship of higher education great "possibilities for love and delight," affirming that "History can teach these things; science can; the social sciences can; and the arts, of course, preeminently can," his application of that shared potential may at times have fallen short with the sciences. Again, Sandra Winicur: "Les is responsible for the suggestion that, since English and History use interlibrary loan, why couldn't the sciences use inter-laboratory loan—there being temporarily unused equipment, he was sure, on other campuses. I tried to explain to him the difficulty of transporting centrifuges and autoclaves, but I don't think he got it. Or wanted to." Though Wolfson may have been a little astigmatic in his perception of the disciplinary needs of the university, his demeanor was never either dismissively regal nor defensively combative. Harold Zisla remembers that there were "stressful issues that Les wouldn't let affect him. Very rarely did he raise his voice or lose his temper. The way I think a normal person would . . . . People loved to come to work. He was very benign." And, despite some disagreement with his judgment, Winicur also says, "When I went in to talk to him, I never felt threatened at all."

A University Becoming

The newness of IUSB and its growing autonomy in the Indiana University system called for a young and largely un-tenured faculty to devote considerable energy to define campus governance, as well as to develop academic programs.

Truth, beauty, goodness, small classes, and a three-course load. These were the principles and practices of the Wolfsonian academy as it emerged from the brambled thicket of a very small, regional university during the decades of the '60s and '70s. Donald Baker at the

University of Colorado told doctoral students in English during the mid-'60s that they might find themselves with appointments at schools that did not yet exist. And my aunts and uncles in Michigan, many of them late in their careers as public school teachers and administrators, when they learned that faculty at IUSB taught three courses two days a week, asked in earnest disbelief whether that was a full-time job.

Defining who we were as an institution and how we would spend our time in and out of the classroom generated a good deal of existential anxiety, committee meetings, and faculty debate during those years. The first four-year degrees were granted in 1967, and the number of tenure-track faculty with a Ph.D. and the number of undergraduate major programs grew exponentially. Would IUSB remain almost exclusively a teaching institution, or would the number of new faculty with research degrees and ambition for publication define the school as a higher-tier research university? By the beginning of the '70s, IU-Bloomington ruled that full-time faculty throughout the system with an incomplete Ph.D. would have two years to finish. Or leave.

Did new faculty coming from doctoral programs into university appointments in the 1960s have a clear sense of the demands of careers in teaching, research, and publication? How much would the quotidian duties of their appointments disable them from teaching well and publishing productively? Some of us certainly chose IUSB because the teaching load of three courses each semester appeared to offer us a productive and mutually nourishing life between, on one hand, the classroom of lectures, discussion, and grading, and, on the other, a library carrel with its shelf of books and journals. Only the major, Tier-I research institutions had teaching loads of only one or two courses per semester. Many state universities—such schools as Ball State University in central Indiana, or Wisconsin State University at Eau Claire—had four-course loads.

The lack of graduate degree programs at IUSB with course work in professors' doctoral specialties restricted opportunities to teach courses complementary to their research. Further, the newness of IUSB and its growing autonomy in the Indiana University system called for a young and largely un-tenured faculty to devote considerable energy to define campus governance, as well as to develop academic programs. Chancellor Wolfson vigorously encouraged the faculty's role in that governance: to form itself as an Academic Senate, to create committees of faculty responsibility, and to write policies and procedures describing the faculty's role in all matters of the academy, including budget, promotion and tenure, curriculum, and student athletics.

In his address to the faculty in September of 1964 (what would become his annual state of the academy address), he said, "A great university cannot exist without a free and vital faculty." Three years later, he qualified that affirmation of faculty freedom when he said that IUSB had "developed a viable faculty organization with as much freedom as is consonant with the proper due of hierarchical order and the bludgeoning of time which causes not only life, but debate, to have a stop." Not all the faculty understood his meaning in that moment, but they would come to realize the necessary limits of their recommendatory power in the years that followed. Departmental chairs and senate committees forwarded their decisions on cases of tenure and promotion to the administration, but even the chancellor's judgment could be overturned in Bloomington by the vice president of regional campuses.

Though there were differences of opinion, most of the faculty believed that their recommendations strongly influenced the chancellor's decisions. In the academic year 1977-1978, the Academic Senate, comprised of all full-time faculty members, debated whether the senate's seven-member Promotion & Tenure Committee ought to report to the chancellor not only its recommendations but its vote count as well. Chancellor Wolfson wanted the vote reported. He attended the meeting at which the senate considered that procedure, participating himself in the debate over which the faculty's elected chair presided. Those proceedings alone testify to the high degree to which he valued open dialogue with the faculty.

The Unbearable Lightness of Teaching

A coherent lecture, a student's luminous insight during a discussion, a memorable blue book essay (saved, then discarded): all of these are evanescent.

Someone years ago said that IUSB had become a good, small liberal arts college, disguised as a regional state university. I think that person was describing the breadth of opportunity for undergraduates that Les Wolfson nurtured. Painting, sculpture, theatre, music, philosophy, creative writing, and foreign languages surrounded degrees in education, dental technology, and business with a richness of humanity. Not everyone understood that. Without dormitories and the social life of fraternities and sororities, and without the tribal energy of pep rallies before football games, some students felt IUSB was not a "real university"; some younger students needed to think of themselves as transients, passing through on their way to IU Bloomington, Purdue, or Notre Dame, but, in the meantime, having to go home to their parents at the end of each day. Non-traditional students, older, with careers and families that bound them to the region, were more likely to discover who Les Wolfson was and to value the choices that IUSB gave them.

Violin lesson with Josef Gingold

Part of the atmosphere of the small liberal arts campus was sustained by small class sizes for freshman and sophomores, far more common at the South Bend campus than at large residential campuses. The pressure of increased enrollments in years when the budget was low could have led to freshmen literature sections of seventy or one-hundred students. Endorsing the importance to critical thinking of classroom discussion and essay exams, the administration allowed the English Department to maintain those classes at thirty-five.

The character and pedagogical dedication of the professor formed, for Les Wolfson, the figure of the illuminating teacher, itself back-lighted by a rich cultural history. Together with the student in the classroom, that shining figure was who Wolfson sought to be, and who he wanted his faculty to be. "Teaching is a science," he mused, "but surely it is even more profoundly an art." Addressing the faculty on the importance of teaching in 1969, Wolfson affirmed that "we are now in pretty substantial agreement that it is no longer possible to maintain that teaching belongs to a cult of unknowability." How we came to know what had been unknowable is not entirely evident, either in his speeches or in my own memory. Only three years before, he had said, "How professors do in their classroom is still the darkest Africa for any evaluator, so we go on evaluating by intuitions, hints, and guesses." Yet he believed that Indiana University intended "to reward good teaching at least as much as it rewards any other academic virtue," which it has done in the decades since with tenure and promotion, as well as many regional and all-university teaching awards that include stipends. Nevertheless, forty years later, researchers continue to explore the old Africa of pedagogy, questioning the professional training of teachers and what constitutes valid evidence of good teaching.

It may be in the nature of our species, or at least of the teaching profession, to declare our classroom failings with more vigorous certainty than we are able to celebrate our successes. And Wolfson, for all his warm hopefulness, could rightly declare our faults. Granting the difficulty of defining education on the fault lines of dissent and controversy in the American '60s and '70s, he saw among us "failures in sympathy," "insufficient generosity," and "fanatics who exude a malign nimbus." In 1970, he believed that the university was in great need of "spiritual continence and restraint." Five years before, even before the social polarization over the Vietnam War, he, a student and practitioner of public discourse, had itemized our classroom deficiencies:

> low-voiced people who make no effort to be heard; drones who deliver everything as if it were of equal weight and import; writers of indecipherable comments; those who demand impossible amounts of work; those who return no papers . . . ; and finally, those who, no matter what they teach,

assume that practically no students they have before them deserve to be in college.

On this last point, Wolfson was provoked by what he regarded as abuses of the grading system, both by faculty with unreasonably high grading standards and by faculty who protested traditional grading on philosophical grounds by awarding the grade of A to everyone.

As it is in all professions, Wolfson could acknowledge the quotidian repetition that is teaching, the discovery we all make every semester of our careers of the daunting sameness of bluebooks. In a 1967 speech, "Tapestries of Afterthought," citing in one paragraph, Dante, C.S. Lewis, and Theodore Roethke, he noted the "tedium," "facelessness," and "indiscernible progress" that is our lot, however punctuated by Elgarian commencements and declarations of future challenges.

He said that teachers must save their students—and themselves—from the dusty death in Roethke's poem, "Dolor":

> I have known the inexorable sadness of pencils, . . .
> All the misery of manila folders and mucilage, . . .
> Ritual of multigraph, paper-clip, comma, . . .
> And I have seen dust form on the walls of institutions, . . .
> Sift, almost invisible, through long afternoons of tedium . . . .

Wolfson knew then what all his friends and colleagues must surely have learned by now and which our successors rediscover every year: the unbearable lightness of teaching. A coherent lecture, a student's luminous insight during a discussion, a memorable blue book essay (saved, then discarded): all of these are evanescent. And yet their aggregate merit must matter, must somehow make an unmeasurable, immeasurable difference in our students, their friends, colleagues, spouses, and children.

From Formalist Theory to Women's Studies

Prior to the '70s, English faculties in higher education had all, or
nearly all, been male, and the literary canon had been almost
exclusively white and Anglo-Saxon.

Research or artistic effort, the adjunct companions to teaching for most faculty at IUSB, held, to Wolfson's mind, neither more merit nor less dolor than the classroom if it merely swelled a bibliography for the sake of promotion or an annual raise. In 1960, in a speech in New York, he warned against meretricious publication: "Nothing can be more absurd than that all actual and incipient college teachers, particularly teachers of speech or English, should have on tap an endless stream of ideas that can be turned into published research. . . . To publish for the sake of publishing . . . is to act in bad faith." Yet he worried about how inept teachers rationalize their lack of ongoing scholarship with claims of having chosen, instead, to be fine teachers; he believed in the necessary responsibility of classroom teachers to maintain and advance their understanding of the major texts of civilization.

What those major texts ought to be changed during Wolfson's tenure as chancellor of IUSB. Prior to the '70s, doctoral study in English, for example, practiced formalist theory in the explication of the grammar, syntax, and prosody of literary texts. English faculties in higher education had all, or nearly all, been male, and the literary canon had been almost exclusively white and Anglo-Saxon. Les Wolfson hired IUSB's first woman tenure-track professor of English, Gloria Kaufman, soon after he came to South Bend, and, during the '70s, she developed courses using women's literature. Her leadership led to a Women's Studies program, with an arts and sciences minor and, by 1991, a major degree. Other developments in literary theory, such as new historicism and deconstruction, emerged during Wolfson's tenure and took their place in the humanities. Before the end of the century, women faculty held tenured positions at IUSB throughout the humanities, as well as in the sciences, behavioral sciences, arts, business, education, and the medical technologies. While Wolfson did not conduct active scholarship in new theories of culture or advocate the curricula of the feminist movement, neither did his administration deny the movement or its academic institutionalization. New ideas and new programs were part of the open discourse of IUSB's culture.

As Long as They Don't Shoot You

Dialogue and public commentary embodied what Wolfson wanted of higher education: an open forum where faculty could air and refine their art and ideas.

Some of the faculty's discussions of general education and major requirements struck Wolfson as all too familiar. Deliberations on the teaching of composition or the requirements of the English major seemed to Wolfson a curricular hamster wheel, the spin of which he observed with amused and patient puzzlement: "Are we still discussing that? I thought that was settled a decade ago."

He preferred to contemplate a wider vision: to the faculty in the fall of 1971, he affirmed the university's difficult responsibility to "honor the expectations of both modern society and the unchangeable expectations of intellectual and aesthetic tradition." Then, and on several occasions, he declared that all disciplines could be gathered into a bipartite curriculum of music and mathematics. "Music," he said, stood for all curricula "directed to man's expressive, affective, and aesthetic dimension," and "mathematics is . . . directed to man's cerebral, ratiocinative, analytical powers . . . at the root of science."

Wolfson's addresses to the faculty appear now like Whitman's career-long revisions of the six editions of *Leaves of Grass*. In many of his speeches, he revisited and glossed earlier speeches. A year later, again to the faculty, he recapitulated his sense of music and mathematics as the two great chambers of curriculum. A colleague had written a reply to his statement of the previous year (Wolfson no longer remembers who that was): "Speaking as a mathematician, I believe that mathematics is a kind of abstract music, and that music is a special kind of mathematics. Therefore, I identify your polar opposites so closely together that they rush into a merger which leaves no room for anything in between." After commenting on that memo (no email in those days), Wolfson agrees that "the two concepts may after all be really only one." He regrets that he had not found opportunities to discuss the subject more, wishing that the Committee on Teaching might explore it during the coming year. That dialogue and public commentary embodied what Wolfson wanted of higher education: an open forum where faculty could air and refine their art and ideas.

He often caromed observations off a colleague's green memo or incidental comment at some campus reception, as when he began one fall address with a reference to the view, not of Peter Piper, but of "a certain sometimes acerbic Serb." How Les Wolfson thought about the university—and the universe in which IUSB hovered nearly undetected—emerged in 1982 with clarity and ironic wholeness in his address to the faculty at large, and to Larry Clipper, English, in particular. Despite the "press of the budgetary vise," the impasse on funding for a new library, and the decline in enrollment growth, Wolfson's speech affirmed the merit of an abiding cheerfulness. Larry Clipper had said to him that Montaigne was wrong to maintain that "the most manifest sign of wisdom is a continual cheerfulness." Wolfson inferred that Clipper believed "perpetual good cheer more often signifies terminal fatuity." He exercised a debater's generosity when he said, "Larry, of course, speaks true." And then he refuted that truth. I have told Les that he seems like the Biblical God in the way that he "giveth and taketh away," but, unlike that God, he does it in a single sentence: "It is a truth on the order of saying that just as profound activity marks the mind of the genius, so something or other is always going on in the mind of the village idiot." Les granted Larry a version of the truth, but he would often refer to him epically as the acerbic Serb and to me as the "hopeless romantic," always paired with some dimension of approval: "Eumaios, O, my swineherd!" Maybe Wolfson's affectionate judgment was kin to the style of the Deep South, where a defamation of character is often followed by a prayerful "Bless his heart!" As our presiding chancellor and cheerful witness, whether talking about math, music, or Montaigne, he always voiced an ironic balance. Harold Zisla remembers how often Les would say about possibility in a culture of violence, "You've got a chance, as long as they don't shoot you."

Goodness of the Human Heart

Despite the 20th century slaughter of two world wars—then wars in Korea and Vietnam, an unrelenting cold war between western democracies and communism, and the terrifying prospect of nuclear war—Wolfson still envisioned a splendor in the campus grass.

That tone of off-handedness about getting shot emanated from Les Wolfson's inexplicably good cheer, given that American leaders were, in fact, being shot: President John Kennedy, in 1963, the year before Wolfson's appointment in South Bend and, five years later, presidential candidate Robert Kennedy and the civil rights leader Martin Luther King, Jr. For Wolfson, despite such painful and destructive national events joined with a controversial war and the polarizing civil rights movement, good cheer had its theoretical ground in the goodness of the human heart, which was itself enhanced by great knowledge. Throughout his tenure at IUSB, he invoked those Wordsworthian, companion virtues as the core of higher education:

> ... The man, whose eye
> Is ever on himself, doth look on one,
> The least of nature's works, one who might move
> The wise man to that scorn which wisdom holds
> Unlawful, ever. O, be wiser thou!
> Instructed that true knowledge leads to love ...
> (*Lyrical Ballads*, 1798, 1800)

His opening address to the faculty acknowledged that such a view was an act of faith, not a provable axiom: "I wish it were possible to prove that there is an inevitable connection between intelligence and character, between formal education and humane endeavor. Some of the ancient Greeks seemed to believe that there was, but experience offers too many examples of the bright and the beautiful who were also the demonic. . . . It is awesome to remember that the devil was once Lucifer, the brightest of the angels." Then, having declared the paradox of Lucifer, he eases "these reservations" aside, imploring his colleagues to keep the faith: "Surely it must be our habitual belief that what Bruno Bettelheim calls the informed heart—good will, speculative intelligence, and practical wisdom working together—should be our total concern in the university."

Despite the 20th century slaughter of two world wars—then wars in Korea and Vietnam, an unrelenting cold war between western democracies and communism, and the terrifying prospect of nuclear war—Wolfson still could see a splendor in the campus grass. He loved the university and wished devoutly that it would be a paradigmatic institution, embodying the ideals of Matthew Arnold, one-hundred years before: "Culture, which is the study of perfection, leads us . . . to conceive of true human perfection as a harmonious perfection, developing all sides of our humanity; and as a general perfection, developing all parts of our society" (*Culture and Anarchy*). He would have the faculty and student body grow into an Arnoldian "happy family," talking out its disagreements civilly and artfully. He cited Arnold Bennett's claim, albeit sentimental, that "a man who really cared for Wordsworth could not possibly kick or curse his old car when it stalled on a steep grade." Or kick or curse a colleague, when that colleague stalled debate on the floor of the Academic Senate.

Year by year, in his annual addresses, Wolfson welcomed the faculty to a "good year," "a glad new year," "one of the brightest years," and "many happy years ahead." Each year, for him, was another season of growth in a progressivist, educational cycle out of "dark inarticulateness," on a "journey to the light."

Music of God

He spoke in Keatsian rhetoric of how he comes to god largely through his "love of the beauty of goodness, and the goodness of beauty" in music.

Of his own interior journey toward some eventual certainty of the spirit beyond the academy, some belief system in or outside of organized religion, Les Wolfson remained, and does remain, always a questioning sensibility, in a state of cheerful unknowing and suspended judgment. He said that the task of teachers is "fundamentally religious," and he expressed on many occasions a consciousness of god. In his 1993 talk at Evangel Heights United Methodist Church, he referenced his lifetime interest in the *Bible* ("King James version preferred!"), the lamentable religious ignorance of students in freshman composition courses, Dante's *Paradiso*, C. S. Lewis, Cardinal Newman, the *Hebrew Bible*, Jesus's Sermon on the Mount, and then concluded that we have been "fashioned by God only a little lower than the angels and crowned with honor and glory." On that occasion, and at other events, he spoke in Keatsian rhetoric of how he comes to god "largely through [his] love of the beauty of goodness, and the goodness of beauty" in music.

He resisted religious text as a narrative of history, with a messiah yet to be born, or to come again, preferring a trans-religious vision, as in Tennyson's belief at the conclusion of *In Memoriam*, in some unspecified "far-off divine event, / To which the whole creation moves." He was intermittent in his attendance at temple, more absent than not, calling himself during one speech in Illinois about Bernard Malamud's fiction, a Jew manqué, defective and unfulfilled; yet, in a congregational meeting at Temple Beth-El in 1993, the occasion of an award to Kurt and Tessye Simon, he affirmed that they did "unceasingly and steadfastly walk in the path of righteousness ordained by the Source of all good."

Wolfson said many times that he had given serious thought of conversion to Roman Catholicism, but it was never clear that it was more than a longing, born of his spiritual appreciation for the abiding truths of another great religion. He was drawn to the power and beauty of what is "caught and celebrated to the limit of human understanding by what is best in our respective faiths." He was well aware of the irony when he said that his spiritual mentor was J. Wesley Robbins, Philosophy, a self-described "disappointed Christian." He recognized the comedic theatre of declaring himself effectively an exile counseled by an exile, but his mind was, at the same time, profoundly engaged in the diversity of contemporary culture and belief, which he repeatedly affirmed.

Penetralium of Mystery

We ought not to discard "a fine isolated verisimilitude caught from the Pen-etralium of mystery," simply because we do not fully understand it.

The glamorous pathos and exile of human consciousness is never more evident than in a university administrator's annual address that proposes to discuss the campus budget in the context of John Keats's notion of the "Penetralium of mystery." I doubt it had ever been done before nor will it be again. Did the faculty gaze at each other "with a wild surmise" that day in 1973? I was there, but I don't remember. No doubt some were vexed by Wolfson's literary prelude to the budget. Some of us may have only half-grasped the transition. Wolfson was warning of the restiveness that the campus felt about the adequacy and fairness of IUSB's share of the Indiana University budget. He urged us to be calm with a Keatsian "content with half-knowledge" and to avoid the neurotic anxiety that the budget would never provide either enough or our fair share. He described "tangles in this thicket" of budgetary appropriation, alluding to possible error in "a formula figure applied to an incorrect base," higher than ordinary service costs, and to the question of legislative intent. Quoting Juliet's profession of boundless love for Romeo, and a somber warning by Tarzan in a TV beer commercial, he assured us that persons of good will were at work throughout the state to fairly appropriate funding for all the state institutions of higher education. Yet he concluded, "Uncertainties, mysteries, and doubts about the total public acceptance of our professional interests will be with us for a long time, perhaps forever."

He advocated as an institutional sensibility the Keatsian capacity "of being in uncertainties, mysteries, doubts without any irritable reaching after fact and reason." We ought not to discard "a fine isolated verisimilitude caught from the Penetralium of mystery," simply because we do not fully understand it. The spirit of mind Wolfson urged on us, and what he saw as the presiding spirit of an open university, is echoed a few years later in Saul Bellow's Nobel Speech of 1976:

> The essence of our real condition, the complexity, the confusion, the pain of it is shown to us in glimpses, in what Proust

and Tolstoy thought of as "true impressions." This essence reveals, and then conceals itself. When it goes away it leaves us again in doubt. But we never seem to lose our connection with the depths from which these glimpses come. The sense of our real powers, powers we seem to derive from the universe itself, also comes and goes.

For all his devotion to the acquisition of knowledge in the academy and its enhancement of the possibility of goodness, Wolfson, in his recognition of the problem of knowing, most fully welcomes the rich immensity of the world. The university, to him, was an open window onto new understandings, backgrounded by an always-receding horizon of certainty. Wolfson's invocation of Keats's sensibility of doubt had its own background in Judaism. In his 1977 lecture on Bernard Malamud's fiction, Wolfson saw in the characters and episodes "an intriguing incompleteness that reflects a typical Jewish strength of not claiming to know more than one can know." The boundary of what one can know is, itself, dim and inexplicable, so it is far easier for a chancellor to live in smiling denial than in the humble recognition, especially on the podium, of uncertainty and the loss that is its companion.

In one address, Wolfson referred to the old philosopher who, hearing only silence in response to his asking, "What is the answer?" paused, and then asked, "In that case, what is the question?" That moment appears in Alice B. Toklas's book, *Someone Says Yes to It*, in which she gives one of her two versions of the last words of Gertude Stein before she died. Les Wolfson's last words?

"What's it all about, Alfie?"

Silence.

"In that case, what's it all about, Alfie?"

Les Wolfson wanted us to join with him to glimpse the vastness of possibility in Indiana University South Bend's small beginnings. If we could not know or have it all, we were not to reject uncertainty. He himself revels in it.

Of the stature of his own achievements, perhaps he is less certain. Les is a contradiction of brilliant, lovable, and self-centered self-effacement. When he came back to campus in the years following his retirement in 1987—to a reception, or to speak at the Wolfson Literary Awards—he liked to say that, unlike the worn phrase, "gone but not forgotten," he, our first chancellor, was "forgotten but not gone." I write this essay in part to say that about that he was wrong.

Bibliography

Wolfson Works:

"Academic Restiveness: Some Thoughts." *Arts and Sciences Review.* Spring, 1959.

Annual Addresses to the Faculty of Indiana University at South Bend, 1964-1986 & Commencement Remarks, 1967-1987.

"Bach and Beatitude." South Bend Chamber Music Concert. January 24, 1971.

"Bess Silverman Wolfson." Eulogy for his mother. December 21, 1984.

"The Cocoa-Nurse." Commencement, Memorial Hospital of South Bend School of Nursing. September 9, 1965.

"D. H. Lawrence and *Lady Chatterley's Lover.*" 1959. IU Northwest.

"Do Not Swell the Rout." IUSB Honor Day Address, IUSB, April 26, 1987.

"An Existentialist View of Research." Convention of the Speech Association of the Eastern States. New York. April 8, 1960.

"For Ted Hengesbach's Retirement." January 13, 2002.

"The Good and the Beautiful in Poetry—from Plato to Dylan Thomas." Indiana University Northwest. Spring, 1960.

"Hats." Undated. Archives, Box 42.

"How Judaism has Shaped my Life." Yom Kippur, 5750. October 9. 1989.

"Inge, O'Neill, and the Human Condition." *The Southern Speech Journal.* Volume XXII. Summer, 1957. No. 4. 221-232.

"Jean Anouilh's Antigone." A review. Undated. Archives, Box 42.

"Jean-Paul Sartre." A review. Undated. Archives, Box 42.

"The Meaning of Merit." Statement for the IUSB Administrative Retreat. March 21, 1983.

"Olga Christine Perschbacher." A eulogy. January, 1990.

"On Poetry." Essay. Undated. Archives, Box 42, File 2.

"On Selecting Subjects for Graduate Research." *Southern Communication Journal.* Volume 20, Issue 1 Autumn 1954.

"Priorities for IUSB." Comments on the report of the 1972 IUSB Committee on Priorities. January, 1974.

"Prologue to Electra." Undated. Archives, Box 42.

"A Rereading of Keats's Odes: the Intrinsic Approach in Literary Criticism." A Prospectus for a Doctoral Dissertation. December, 1949.

"*Romeo and Juliet*: Program Notes." IUSB Campus Theatre. April, 1965.

"The Road for College Education." English 71 paper, University of Michigan. Spring, 1944.

Rycenga, John A., and Wolfson, Lester M. "Religion and the College Student." *The Newman Review*. Wayne State University. First Quarter, 1963.

"Season of Faith and Hope." Evangel Heights United Methodist Church, South Bend, Indiana. March 10, 1993.

"Should the Reform Congregation Adopt a Written Guide of Ritual Practices?" Delivered for a debate in Houston, Texas. Spring, 1955.

"Shylock." Shakespeare Fortnight, IUSB. October 23, 1985.

"The Still, Sad Music." Mayor's United Nations Dinner. October 23, 1974.

"The Stranger." Book Review of Camus. *University of Michigan Perspectives*. January, 1947.

"Suffering and Love: The Fiction of Edward Lewis Wallant." Adult Study Group of the South Bend Jewish Council. January 12, 1966.

"The Tapestries of Afterthought." Gary English Council Annual Banquet. April 20, 1967.

"Temple Beth-El Congregational Meeting." Address as President of the Kurt and Tessye Simon Foundation. June 16, 1993.

"Top Lines and Low Tech." Phi Beta Kappa Address, Notre Dame. May 17, 1986.

"The Vision of the Impossible." Address at Bethel College. Box 42, Folder 3, 1 of 3. Wolfson Publications, Speeches, & Writings. Delivered at Bethel College, May 22, 1967.

"Wolfson-Nixon Letters." May 5, 1970, June 24, 1970.

"The Wondering and Wandering Jew in Malamud's Fiction." Third Annual Scholars in Residence Program, Congregation Solel, Highland Park. Illinois. March 11-13, 1977.

"Zisla Hall of Fame Induction Address." Century Center. May 6, 1990.

Works of Others:

Collins, Walt R. "Education . . . as the Best Hope of Civilization." *Indiana Alumni Magazine.* April, 1971.

Demaree, Robert W., Jr. "Demaree Letter of Support for honorary degree of Doctor of Humane Letters." December 29, 1987.

Zisla, Harold. "Induction of Lester Wolfson into South Bend Hall of Fame." 1991.

"Vale, Dr. Wolfson." *South Bend Tribune.* 1987.

"Wolfson Colloquium." Conversations among faculty, remembering the Wolfson years. IUSB, May, 2008.

Lester Wolfson in his second floor Schurz Library office

The Wolfson Papers

Addresses to the Faculty
and Graduates

A Hope for the South Bend Campus
Delivered at a faculty meeting,
September 19, 1964

Recognizing life's imponderables, especially in teaching, Wolfson joyfully advocates for the academy an informed heart—good will, speculative intelligence, and practical wisdom. The university's faculty and students should articulate that model for an informed society.

Let me begin by expressing my deep appreciation for the kindness and co-operation I have received throughout the summer from the officers, faculty, and staff with whom I have worked. Today I see and meet most of you for the first time, and have no adequate words to state my pleasure at the prospect of serving Indiana University with you in the future.

An old saying has it that "all beginnings are difficult." That my beginning at the South Bend Campus was not difficult at all can be attributed only to the cordiality with which I have been received. For that, I am truly in your debt, and hope that your gracious reception will extend to forgiving me for reading a manuscript rather than speaking spontaneously. I assure you that the spontaneous feelings are abundantly there, but my problem is that for the first time in thirty-six years I am forsaking the classroom. (Before anyone thinks that I am older than I look, I should say that the thirty-six years are reckoned from my kindergarten days.) Leaving the classroom—at least temporarily—I fear that unless I seize every opportunity to articulate my thoughts as precisely as possible, you will soon be shaking your heads sadly that yet another passing-fair faculty member has dwindled into administration.

If my beginning on July 1 was not difficult, my effort to begin these remarks has been. Perhaps it is because the fall season is such a curiously mixed time for an academician: the air becomes bracing; there is a new crop of students who, hopefully, will be better than last year's; *we* will be better than last year—all our dampened enthusiasms reawakened, all our lost opportunities to teach and learn renewed yet once again. For us, it is a tonic time, but—if we think closely on how important our calling is—it is also a sober time.

You will understand how this mixed feeling is further compounded for me personally today. None of you will have been deceived that the neutral "A" in my title, "A Hope for the South Bend Campus," is in reality anything other than my hope for the South Bend Campus. In fact, I would have honestly announced my subject in that way if there wasn't such a silly ring to it: though there is probably no danger of anyone's mistaking me for a Miss America candidate, like you I have suffered through too many vapid personal utterances—for public display—on high-sounding words like "sincerity," "philosophy," and "hope" itself. Yet we all know that these words do have glorious meanings if we can free them from all the distortions lent by ignorance and false sentiment.

In a celebrated passage in *A Farewell to Arms* Ernest Hemingway wrote:

> I was always embarrassed by the words sacred, glorious, and sacrifice and the expression in vain. We had heard them . . . now for a long time, and I had seen nothing sacred, and the things that were glorious had no glory and the sacrifices were like the stockyards at Chicago if nothing was done with the meat except to bury it. There were many words that you could not stand to hear and finally only the names of places had dignity. . . . Abstract words such as glory, honor, courage, or hallow were obscene beside the concrete names of villages, the numbers of roads, the names of rivers, the numbers of regiments and the dates.

Hemingway is protesting the slaughter and the hypocrisies of World War I, but he is also saying something larger about human character and language. Safe, abstract words frequently cloak mean thoughts and motives. And such words are most pernicious when the user fools himself more than he does others. Since I am trying to deliver what in the main will be a solemn speech—the occasion being what it is—I hope I will not be guilty of fooling myself by using large words loosely.

Apart from the danger of hollow pontificating presented by any serious occasion, there is the second difficulty of trying to say anything fresh about higher education. A speaker who talks about even a small part of so demanding a subject runs a risk of grave presumption. A very funny routine at a Chicago cabaret called Second City presents a mock-philosopher with the deliberately improbable name of Walther von der Vogelweide who delivers a monologue entitled "A Short Talk on the Universe." When an imagined heckler asks him why he chose such a subject, he answers, "What other subject is there?" I feel that a short talk on education is like a short talk on the universe—it is the only subject, and yet it is bound to fail because the topic cannot readily be defined.

A last difficulty for me is that there are always the imponderables: some of you have heard of the dying philosopher whose grieving friends were gathered around his bed. At length the moribund old sage raised himself painfully from his pallet, shook his fist at the heavens, and cried out, "What is the answer?" Sinking back, he appeared dead, until raising himself yet one more time, he shook his fist and cried, "What is the question?" For us as teachers, perhaps the imponderables are best summed up by an adaptation a friend of mine once made of two Edwin Arlington Robinson poems. Blending Richard Cory and Miniver Cheevy into Miniver Cory, my friend's poem concluded:

> And Miniver Cory, one calm summer night,
> Went home and put a bullet through his head,
> And went on teaching.

But if there are recurring problems in teaching that confront us at every turn, and if we often feel ambivalent about what we are doing, surely the mark of an able faculty is its unremitting devotion to the honorable task of accumulating, refining, and transmitting all the knowledge of mind, sense, and heart accessible to human comprehension. Whether our particular interest leads us to deal primarily with words, gestures, formulas, lines, colors, musical notes, or ritual enactments, we should all be concerned that our students have as complete a grasp as possible of the methods, presuppositions, limitations, prospects, and leading achievements in all the disciplines that lend themselves to intellectual and imaginative understanding.

If this is our task, it is equally, and concomitantly, our joy. I wish it were possible to prove that there is an inevitable connection between intelligence and character, between formal knowledge and humane endeavor. Some of the ancient Greeks seemed to believe that there was, but experience offers too many examples of the bright and the beautiful who were also the demonic. Whether we view Satan literally or symbolically, it is awesome to remember that the devil was once Lucifer, the brightest of the angels.

But all these reservations aside, surely it must be our habitual belief that what Bruno Bettelheim calls the informed heart—good will, speculative intelligence, and practical wisdom working together—should be our total concern in the University. And though it is fanatical to insist that a given life style is the only acceptable one, is it too much to say that our zeal for our studies and our hope that our students may share that zeal is created by what we know of the joyous light that understanding gives? Arnold Bennett was somewhat sentimental when he claimed that a man who *really* cared for Wordsworth could not possibly kick or curse his old car when it stalled on a steep grade; but if learning *can* resign us to stalled cars, more positively it can lead us to more charitable and sensitive human encounters. Whatever our specialties, it must be our common faith as educated people that every advance learning helps us to make over our desert spaces within, our dark inarticulateness, represents a journey to the light, to order imposed on chaos. Seeing that light, realizing our full humanity, is intensely pleasurable, and that pleasure—that joy—is the necessary precondition for human love. These, I believe, are the things that school and college are really all about, not—as in our statistical anonymity we often seem to suggest—about credits and grades, majors and minors, requirements and electives.

I know that I may be guilty of reckless question begging when, holding that the real indignities to men come from willful malice, apathetic neglect, and an inordinate desire for power and personal comfort, I argue further that *truly* educated people cannot be proud, brutal, indifferent, or neglectful. We will survive only through learning to live humanly in a precarious world. Though many of you will disagree, in my view the college and university will play a larger part in guaranteeing that survival than will be played by any other institution. If there is no necessary connection between character and intellect, I am sure that there is a high positive correlation and that the rational orderings we discover and transmit as university people will translate themselves into the personal and social orderings that mark a warm and generous society.

The great university, in its perfection, is a model for that warm and generous society. Since the end of World War II, Indiana University has grown in distinction until it is beyond question one of the most eminent universities in our country. The South Bend Campus is an integral and inseparable part of Indiana University. Given the obvious differences in scope, everything that is wished for and expected of our largest campus is wished for and expected of our South Bend Campus.

Those of us who have been members of the regional campus system for five, ten, fifteen or more years have witnessed remarkable development, particularly in the last five—even the last two—years. In reading very recent announcements and publications, you know what rapid expansion is immediately before us—the legislature willing. So long as it is accompanied by quality, growth is to be welcomed for the simple reason that it will enable us to do better the things that we can do well now. More books, more journals, more equipment, more colleagues, more complete programs, more full-time students—all these things will give us greater cohesion and greater opportunities for gladly learning and teaching than we have ever known here before. As matters become firm enough to report on in confident, specific detail, I pledge to you that I will inform you as quickly and as fully as I can.

But while we rightly look forward to these developments, we should not minimize what we have now and what remains to be done even if we were never to grow larger. If Faust could say to the passing moment, "Stay, thou art so fair," and if sufficient unto the day is the evil thereof, so also sufficient unto the day are the opportunities thereof. At our next few meetings, I want to present systematically for your consideration some half-dozen suggestions that may make *this* year at the South Bend Campus a better year. I will not elaborate on any of these suggestions at the moment, but would like to touch on some of them briefly.

First, and to my mind far and away foremost, I should like to see the faculty evolve the machinery whereby its voice in policy matters can be heard loud and clear. As an adjunct to that, I would hope that any committee, whether administratively appointed or created by an organized faculty, will feel free to work as far as its collective talents and energies will permit without worry about being second-guessed or reversed from above. It is a truism that a great university cannot exist without a free and vital faculty.

Second, I should like to see the students organize with verve—even with what to some may seem daring. Weak institutions are those that feel themselves above criticism. To be sure, it is our responsibility to set proper limits and to provide the best examples of dignity and restraint that we can. Yet we should not be afraid of being shot at verbally. I am not suggesting that we encourage insurrection, but a vital faculty presupposes (and creates) a vital student body. We should not only expect, but should actually welcome, the problems that independent student activities always present as these young people take their measure and find their space.

Third, I would hope that our splendid theater will soon prove too small rather than too large. We must use every legitimate way we can to convince our students that drama and film and painting and music are necessary complements to what they read in their literature classes, and the means to the harmonious development of their highest affective powers.

At other times, I will have more to suggest as to how we can serve the community at large in ways appropriate to our university standing; as to how we can turn our relative smallness to interdisciplinary advantage; as to how we can provide for the special skills of our superior students; as to how we can encourage adults to take up or to continue educations long since neglected or abandoned.

If all these are worthy aims, I believe it is apparent that they can be best realized only in an atmosphere of absolute magnanimity and trust. Later, when you read the faculty handbooks distributed today, you will notice a section abstracted from the all-University handbook.

The section is concerned with the ethics of faculty relations. I hope that none of us will deny the importance of our treating with public respect all facets of our University operation—both here and at Bloomington. I am not suggesting that we become company men, or that none of the University programs is beyond improvement. Perhaps some programs should be seriously modified or even abolished. (I, for example, have no sympathy with the disproportionate attention given to intercollegiate athletics.)

But as we try to walk the line between private conviction and public stance, we may sometimes wonder how anyone can be an administrator or even be a cooperating member of a department. There is always the nagging doubt that conciliation and compromise are really betrayals of principle or disguises for lack of courage. Yet if faults sometimes seem to abound, we should remember that we are members of a major university which has men of courage and principle in crucial positions. In such a university, incompetence and inefficiency find it difficult to establish a foothold.

If there *is* any danger in a major university, inefficiency is far more likely than incompetence. Here I am thinking of the kind of crippling that occurs when factions, cliques, rump sessions, and splinter groups of all sorts weaken faculty effort by directing energies away from scholarship, teaching, and public service. There are third-rate colleges, with both incompetence and inefficiency the rule, where some of the worst aspects of a certain public school mentality prevail. Deans prowl the halls looking through the windowed doors of classrooms to check up on God knows what; the few good faculty members are harassed by reactionary groups with such grandiose names as Minute Women. But I know, also, strong—even distinguished—departments that have been hobbled from within by vindictiveness, spleen, and simple lack of charity. It is hard to calculate how much is lost if one lives in an academic atmosphere of averted glances and slamming doors when the "wrong" person comes down the corridor.

In my few months at the South Bend Campus, practically every evidence leads me to be confident that we can have an academic association that is at once highly intelligent and generously motivated. So that none of that force is dissipated, on my part I will do all that I can to act on your wishes wherever possible. If questions arise that cannot be resolved locally, I will instantly seek the counsel of those elsewhere who may resolve them. Our single purpose as a staff working together, whether as senior professors or the most recently hired clerks, is to invest every detail of our appointed tasks with the thoroughness, the care, and the excellence that is represented by Indiana University as a whole. There is enough in the world at large that is shoddy, haphazard, and mean without our adding anything to that dismal store.

In full awareness that Hemingway's ghost may be cautioning from the wings, I will venture to say that although we are a secular institution, we have a sacred charge. We hear so much about climbing enrollments and how necessary college is to help one's life income that we may forget that we are really concerned with something quite different from the quantitative. Whatever our particular discipline, our passion for intellectual order is akin to all other concerns for the spirit. One of the most exquisite sensibilities of our time put it beautifully in considering the forces and persons that had shaped his life—forces and persons that shape our lives too as scholars, teachers, and complete beings. Let me end by reading Stephen Spender's "I Think Continually of Those Who Were Truly Great."

> I think continually of those who were truly great.
> Who, from the womb, remembered the soul's history
> Through corridors of light where the hours are suns,
> Endless and singing. Whose lovely ambition
> Was that their lips, still touched with fire,
> Should tell of the spirit clothed from head to foot in song.
> And who hoarded from the spring branches
> The desires falling across their bodies like blossoms.
>
> What is precious is never to forget
> The delight of the blood drawn from ageless springs
> Breaking through rocks in worlds before our earth;
> Never to deny its pleasure in the simple morning light,
> Nor its grave evening demand for love;
> Never to allow gradually the traffic to smother
> With noise and fog the flowering of the spirit.

Near the snow, near the sun, in the highest fields
See how these names are fêted by the waving grass,
And by the streamers of white cloud,
And whispers of wind in the listening sky;
The names of those who in their lives fought for life,
Who wore at their hearts the fire's center.
Born of the sun they traveled a short while towards the sun,
And left the vivid air signed with their honor.

Remarks to the Faculty
Indiana University at South Bend,
September 21, 1968

In a review of IUSB's early years of night classes in South Bend Central High School, Wolfson acknowledges the campus's still amorphous identity. He calls for new academic definition and vision to develop a campus that has always sustained the integrity of Indiana University. He outlines serious problems in higher education, while noting instances of creative growth at IUSB.

Since September is the month when the heralding angles glorify the new automobiles, and since September 1968 is the month when "the real Nixon" seeks to unmask "the real Humphrey," we are at a special time when people who respect language know how easy it is for credibility gaps to become credibility chasms. Accordingly, I shall try to be temperate and circumspect, though I do not want to repress my personal enthusiasm at the prospect for Indiana University at South Bend this year and in the years to come. That enthusiasm is born from both my direct thirteen-year knowledge of men and movements within Indiana University, and from a reading many of us here assembled give to emerging new emphases that mark the entire span of American education.

In relating that knowledge and that reading to our immediate local situation, I think it follows that we can speak sense about the freshly-named Indiana University at South Bend if we see our campus as not only a happy consequence of our institutional past, but also as a somewhat amorphous new entity on the verge of possible definition in the light of a transcendently envisioned future.

Let me focus my remarks this morning by dwelling briefly on that past and on that future. I will not say much about the present since its character can best be known as each of you now feels it, or soon will feel it, on your pulse of mood and judgment.

Robert Robinson, Administrative Assistant and Instructor in Accounting,
1957-58, teaches a class offered at Central High

Only 8 of our current full-time professional staff of 90 antedate my own arrival in South Bend in 1964, and only 3 of those 8—Professors de Lara, Robinson, and Sudermann—have extensive personal knowledge of the way it was in the many years when the old South Bend-Mishawaka Center operated in sardine-can intimacy at Central High School. The almost exclusively part-time evening students of the 1940s and 1950s were served by a small number of full-time instructors, varying for most of those years between six and twelve. The bulk of the instructional program was taught by part-time faculty composed mainly of business and professional people in the community, but supplemented by Bloomington faculty who drove (and later flew by University plane) to South Bend on a weekly basis. Although occasional classes had been taught in South Bend before 1940, the first resident director of the Center was named in that year, and 1940 can be considered the beginning of our formal existence as an institution.

Although two years of credit work applicable to Indiana University degrees were allowed during most of our early history, a study made in 1955 showed that few students in fact completed more than one year at the various Indiana University Centers around the state. This can undoubtedly be explained by the paucity of courses and by the unprepossessing facilities—probably in equal measure.

The old University Centers had two main functions: one was to provide for commuter and working students the limited credit program just mentioned; the other was to provide a series of non-credit lectures and short courses to the community. The importance and early scope of the second function was reflected in the name our Division carried at various stages: "The Division of Adult Education and Public Services," which alternated with the name "The Division of University Extension" until 1966, when "The Division of Regional Campuses" was officially created. The extension centers of the '40s and '50s, and those that existed much earlier in Fort Wayne and Indianapolis, had their staunch defenders and dedicated pioneer staff. But because of their smallness and general invisibility, they were sometimes referred to individually, even by those who loved them with fond irreverence, as "The Stench." Despite this, in those first days, the crucial character of the IU branches was being shaped by continuous resolution on the part of University and Divisional administrative officers that, ill-favored as we in some respects were, *all* Indiana University programs throughout the state would have the integrity connoted by the Indiana University name. To that end, the established comprehensive departments and schools at Bloomington have always been involved in the appointment, retention, promotion, and related professional decisions affecting the state-wide faculty. The extent of input from Bloomington has varied from department to department, and even within the same department from era to era, but the over-all relationship has established a pattern of expectation and perquisite which provides us with a sound base for making the ever more autonomous decisions we will be called upon to make in the years immediately to come.

Until 1965, operating funds for the regional campuses were derived almost exclusively from fee income, with a small percentage of the total budget being siphoned off from the Bloomington budget. In 1965, concurrent with announcement of plans for the initial degree programs at Gary and South Bend, the first modest direct legislative appropriations for regional operating costs were made. Those amounts were substantially increased in 1967, although both the lag in general understanding that essentially new colleges were being created in the urban areas of the state, and the fiscal problems relating to tax base and to the citizenry's scale of values have joined to make 1968-69 a tight time for us and indeed for the entire University. (I might say, parenthetically, that this sense of sudden halt has understandably led some of us to short temper and to a feeling that there is a subtle betrayer lurking about somewhere if only we could find him. There is no betrayer. The reason we went from 85 full-time appointments in 1967 to only 90 in 1968, after a much larger advance the year before, is simply that there were no funds to do more. Perhaps some encouragement can be found in recalling that our 26 member full-time staff of 1964 served 2,000 credit students and we now have 90 serving 3,400 credit students in 1968, a significant gain even after allowing for the present much larger number of full-time students.)

From the quiet beginnings just sketched we came, then, to the critical degree-program turning-point in 1965. By that time, we had occupied our own first building for four years, and were a year away from occupying Greenlawn Hall. We had also begun purchasing the houses on the perimeter of our present campus, houses which will some day be torn down (as even in all likelihood will be Greenlawn Hall itself) and replaced by permanent structures as we implement the physical site master plan currently being devised by professional landscape and building architects. Our programmatic master plan, first drawn up in 1966, revised in 1968, and scheduled for flexibly conceived revision every two years, is the basic document which systematically projects our development. All the full-time staff have, or should have, copies of the 1968 version, and extra copies will be placed in the Library for the use of associate faculty who may be interested.

With the degree commitments made in 1965 came further developments in faculty and administrative structure already begun on a slight scale a few years before. For many years, most of the old Centers had one administrative officer—the Director—maybe two officers if you count the Academic Counselors, who were half-time faculty members and half-time factotums with more duties than ever Figaro had. And if Mario Savio's view that administrators are necessary only to keep the sidewalks clean has a modicum of truth, he would have particularly valued the old-time Directors, who I hear, perhaps apocryphally, used to change the light bulbs, refill the dispensers, and sweep out the lobbies. At South Bend, our aforementioned extensive non-credit program had its own administrator, and in the 1960s an assistant director was responsible for many academic and certain financial matters.

It was not until 1964 that a regional campus faculty member was first named "assistant chairman" of a liberal arts department, and since that time we have been moving rapidly toward assuming both the shape and substance of a complete collegiate, even university, pattern. A most dramatic impetus was given to this growth last April by President Stahr's recommendation that the University be considerably decentralized with an eye toward eventual establishment of seven autonomous campuses within a confederation of Indiana University campuses, each one—including Bloomington—to be headed by a Chancellor.

President Stahr's recommendation was approved by the Trustees in June of this year, and on July 1 our name was officially changed from the South Bend-Mishawaka Campus of Indiana University to Indiana University at South Bend. For the time being, the campuses at South Bend, Gary, Fort Wayne, Kokomo, and Jeffersonville continue to be thought of in somewhat similar ways, and have reporting responsibility to the new Vice-President for Regional Campuses, Dr. John W. Ryan, former Chancellor of the University of Massachusetts at Boston. Dr. Ryan plans to make an early trip to South Bend to meet the faculty and staff, to seek your views directly, and to share with you some of his own.

Although substantial formal change will mark our near future, in keeping with the modest gains in total staff this year, we have made only two changes, although extremely important ones, in administrative structure. With the appointment of Dr. Donald D. Snyder, Associate Professor of Physics, as Chairman of the newly formed Division of Arts and Sciences we hope to give more coherence to our most complex academic unit, to discover increasingly effective recruiting techniques, to expedite the formal organization of departments, to hasten the planning of solid degree programs, to create clearer lines of internal reporting, and to develop improved ways of assessing professional merit. In the early weeks of the semester, Dr. Snyder will be in touch with the Arts and Sciences faculty, and particularly with the Assistant Chairmen, for the purpose of establishing working procedures.

A major change of the past few years has been the development of a corps of student affairs officers, working with Dean Beutler in the critical tasks of admissions, high-school liaison, freshman orientation, record keeping, counseling, and general supervision of student activities. Now a comparable development in business affairs has been achieved in the appointment of Mr. Otis S. Romine as the first Business Manager of Indiana University at South Bend. Mr. Romine's main responsibilities will be to assist the faculty in the requisitioning, locating, purchasing, and placing of supplies and equipment; to work with Dean Risler and myself in the preparation of the annual budget; to supervise, with appropriate delegation, the maintenance and clerical staff (whose full-time numbers have grown from 19 in 1964 to 45 in 1968 and will double again in due order); and finally, to use his extensive engineering and Guatemalan voodoo knowledge to help keep our buildings safe from witches, warlocks, and the kinds of harm inflicted by the monsoon rains of June 25!

So that, in rough outline, is where we are at the moment. I hope this brief account of how we have gotten to this point has given perspective, particularly to our new colleagues. Before I turn to other things, let me introduce the eighteen new full-time members of our professional staff, welcome them most cordially, and say how pleased we are to have their strength. In alphabetical order, they are:

> Dr. Harold J. Babrov, Associate Professor of Physics
> Dr. Hansom P. Baptiste, Jr., Assistant Professor of Education
> Stephen S. Denner, Lecturer in Sociology
> James B. Eckstein, Director of the Computing Center
> Robert L. Keyser, Assistant to the Business Manager
> Charles P. Lehman, Lecturer in Speech and Theatre

Eugene E. Love, Assistant to the Dean of the Junior
    Division
Dr. Joseph E. Morrow, Assistant Chairman, and Assistant
    Professor of Psychology
Edward M. Palumbo, Lecturer in English
Otis S. Romine, Business Manager
Dr. Eldon E. Ruff, Assistant Professor of Education
Dr. Earl J. Savage, Assistant Professor of Botany
Dr. Richard S. Schlunt, Assistant Professor of Mathematics
Dr. Roy E. Schreiber, Assistant Professor of History
Barry M. Scott, Reference Librarian
Dr. John R. Swanda, Jr., Assistant Professor of Business
    Administration
William H. Tibbetts, Admissions Officer
John J. Weger, Lecturer in Business Administration

I was not aware until I reviewed what I have said the past four
September how, in one way or another, the talk always got around to
teaching. What I have just sketched about our development basically
describes only machinery. Although the desire to grow numerically,
to add more programs, to achieve neater organization is natural and
good—all these things in themselves—statistics, hierarchy, image,
scope—are empty, or worse, unless some qualitative spirit breathes
through every encounter we have with our students. Student unrest on
hundreds of campuses these past few years has called into question the
relevance of what we are doing—not only for the student, but for the
larger world both they and we must share.

Near the beginning of my remarks I mentioned the reading some
of us give to emerging new emphases in the entire span of American
education, and I suggested that we could define *our* institution, if we
wished, in the light of a transcendently envisioned future. The absur-
dity of paradoxes long insisted upon has now been clearly discerned:
we tell college students they are adults, and treat them otherwise; in
too many of our humanities and social science programs we tell them
they should think for themselves, and grade them by our dogmatisms,
or else create an atmosphere in which they cannot flourish; in beginning courses, we try to apprentice them to our idiosyncratic interests

and then fail to understand why they are so unappreciative. In short, too many teachers violate the dignity of their students by being contemptuous of the young, by forgetting, as the fine poet and teacher Theodore Roethke states it,

> that they themselves did not spring fully mature from the brow of Jove: they forget the vast patience of others who labored for them, often unbeknownst to them. Arrogance, in our profession, is an understandable sin, especially when one considers the brutalization, the crassness of much of contemporary life . . . the dead pall that hangs over the spirit. But it is nonetheless, a sin.

Roethke describes that arrogance as coming from the "frightened or unsure who cover up their grinding sense of inadequacy by the austere false front," or from "bright young men who spend all their time being right; brisk, metallic, negative intelligences." At an earlier level, as Jonathan Kozol recounts it in his book *Death at an Early Age*, there is the art teacher who crumbles the exploratory drawing effort of a painfully withdrawn ghetto child and calls it garbage because it does not conform to the teacher's notion of "acceptable" line, form, and color.

Where, in their training, did the scholars and the teachers from whom the students feel so estranged get the notion that their formal credentials permit them to use psychic truncheons against the student's unsteady and vacillating desire to learn? Or why should the bright young men feel that they are somehow diminished if they bend to the student instead of derricking him to their own rarefied height, probably choking him in the process? Undoubtedly, until we know a great deal more about motivation, and even after we know it, there will be some students who cannot or will not learn, but in our legitimate fear of weakening genuine standards, why do we feel there is no better way of teaching and learning than to assign passing or failing grades for good or poor performance over so short a time as three or four months? God Himself countenances many falls from grace but most colleges allow only one fall from grades. It is amazing that so few have seen the implications of the successes achieved with "high risk" (academically marginal and sub-marginal) students through compensatory training and some willingness to modify the respect rather arbitrarily given to upper middle-class standards of "literacy." We can give compensatory training of sorts in our own classroom by redoubling efforts that may have become casual or cavalier, and by asking ourselves if we have unconsciously developed elitist notions that will, through his failure which *may* be ours, prevent our student from gaining in his measure the particular sensitivity any decent college education makes possible.

Too often we commit what Karl Menninger, in an even more forgiving context, has recently called "the crime of punishment." In our schools and colleges, we punish slowness and uncertainty of purpose, which can hardly be considered crimes. We become so anxious to locate ourselves and our students within such a carefully delimited range on the spectrum of human ability and accomplishment that we forget that the only significant special cases may well be, at one end, the extreme defective who will need complete care all his life; and at the other end a Shakespeare or Einstein, who outtop knowledge. By what strange kind of self-granted dispensation do we ever justify being callous or indifferent to the students in our care? The fearsome academic and loss-of-interest mortality rate in our colleges can only in part be attributed to the non-academic motives that still bring many—maybe most—young people to college. Surely much of it must come from their restiveness at what they find not sufficiently large, or generous, or humane.

In a recent article by theologian Michael Novak, the author reveals, I think, profound understanding of how the

> young dissident who is not to become corrupted by his "pure" conviction that "the system," provides no knowledge about how to become a genuine human being in our age must learn that "purity," in order not to be destructive, must be tempered by forgiveness, gentleness, a sense of one's own dishonesties, a recognition of other human ideals—even of bourgeois, middle-class, and coalitionist ideals.

If I may extend one of Novak's implications, I would suggest that the "pure" professor—us—

who is not to be corrupted by his "pure" conviction that
the young dissident provides no knowledge about how to
become a genuine human being in our age must learn that
"purity," in order not to be destructive, must be tempered
by forgiveness, gentleness, a sense of one's own dishonesties,
a recognition of other human ideals—even of iconoclastic,
classless, and individualistic ideals.

In short, Novak suggests that the confrontations racking university campuses today are caused by fundamental failures in sympathy, by lack of imaginative power on both sides, by young people's not knowing they can learn from the past, and our not knowing we can learn from the current temper. What to do about these rifts once they have occurred is, of course, quite another problem, and we will soon be witnessing many new efforts to solve it—not, I hope, here.

A few decades ago, graduate students in literary criticism were talking, in the jargon of the time, about "the intentional fallacy," "the affective fallacy," and "the fallacy of misplaced concreteness." Following Novak, perhaps we can coin our own phrase, "the fallacy of misplaced purity," and define it as the fallacious notion that rigidly following an unbending obsessive standard or attitude or pattern will lead to wisdom, fame, authority, justice, etc.—or, at the very least, to a warming sense of one's personal probity. It is notions like this, in various insidious forms, that lead to the sterility and frantic boredom of so many classrooms.

The fallacy of misplaced purity would have prevented Mike Esselstrom from developing a project in music education that brings music to deprived children in ways both therapeutic and aesthetic. It would have told Virginia Harvin and Mary Gilchrist that arithmetic methods is one thing, and language arts methods another, so that there was no sense in their organizing their sections to teach the same group of students. It would have told Don Snyder that physics is for the upper 10% of students, and since special intellectual power is necessary to comprehend the subject, that there was no point in devising a special course for the non-science oriented average student. Don will soon publish a paper demonstrating quite the opposite. It would have told several of our liberal arts departments and our Division of Education that there can be no common cause between the "purity" of the liberal arts and the "practicality" of Education, and we would not have our special courses organized ready to be of use to in-service elementary teachers. It might have questioned our Department of History on its team teaching of lectures in basic history courses with discussion sections led individually by a professor who shares in the lectures.

These first innovations at our campus, and the earlier use of some of them at other campuses throughout the country, are only the forerunners of courses, sequences, workshops, and institutes that will serve not only our regular students but which will bring our corporate talents directly into the city and will bring the city to us. The artificial divisions long fostered between the intellectual community and the larger political community; or between the business world, the arts and sciences, and the service professions, will increasingly be bridged.

If we and other nations survive the Vietnam War, and if we avoid the ultimate polarizations which are caused by all those who refuse to recognize how deep we are bound in our common humanity, there will be means, and time, and desire, and strength for us and other emerging universities to make major contributions to these good ends of human harmony. As the democratic ideal is at last fully realized in our schools and colleges, the things done there, not only in keenness of mind, but also in amplitude of heart and elevation of spirit, will be the true wonders of our earth.

May we all have a good year.

Remarks
Third Annual
Commencement Exercises

Northside Hall Auditorium, June 4, 1969

In the wake of the recent, tragic assassinations of Robert Kennedy and Martin Luther King, Jr., we see more clearly how we must live by "the acts and arts of civility."

C hancellor Wells, Vice-President Ryan, Mr. Lucas, colleagues, graduating students, ladies and gentlemen:
    A year ago, the second annual commencement ceremonies of Indiana University at South Bend were held as Senator Robert Kennedy lay dying in a California hospital. Only a few months before that, Martin Luther King had also been cruelly slain by an attitude the antithesis of everything civilized. On the occasion of Dr. King's death, a good portion of the South Bend faculty wrote a kind of letter to the world in which they said, among other things:

> . . . we want laws designed to give everyone complete equality. . . . We want to guarantee a job to every man who wants to work. We want to guarantee an education to everyone who wants to learn. We want to guarantee, against a society which has taught despair, the possibility for hope. . . . We want to send armies to the cities this summer, not with guns but with shovels, not to suppress but to encourage, not to die but to live and to love and to build . . . nurseries and community centers

and libraries and schools and hospitals and homes. The time for words is long past. We have all had too much of hating and of killing and of despair. Now is the time for positive programs, for imaginative and fearless programs. Now is the time for legislators to act strongly and justly as our representatives. Now is the time—today—this hour—this minute!

The passion of that cry from many deeply responsible people, coupled with its implicit insistence on a need for faith in the democratic process, is shared by ever-larger numbers of students and citizens who also have a dream of a fuller human life. But dramatic assassinations, let alone less spectacular acts of material hurting, are a tragically dear price to pay for sharpening our uncertain awareness of how dependent our happiness is on cultivation of gentleness and affection and respect—in short, a cultivation of all the acts and arts of civility.

Wherever education fails, it fails most when it ignores civility, and rests content in producing trained functionaries or quick-tongued disputants who are fortified in their native arrogance. It is fashionable in some quarters these days to think that rudeness is a mark of honesty and blunt plain-speaking, while politeness is a mask for privilege or an insidious co-opting grace. To think in this manner, by failing to see the similarity between gross acts of overt violence and less direct ways of eroding effective self-assurance is to contribute to an atmosphere in which no man or nation can truly flourish.

Although there is perhaps something a little quaint about Cardinal Newman's classic definition of the gentleman, it should still be persuasive to anyone whose education has helped him to know not only the strength but also the limits of his understanding—his informed heart:

> . . . a gentleman . . .is one who never inflicts pain. . . . He has his eyes on all company; he is tender towards the bashful, gentle towards the distant, and merciful towards the absurd. . . . He makes light of favors while he does them, and seems to be receiving when he is conferring . . . he has no ears for slander or gossip, is scrupulous in imputing motives to those who interfere with him, and interprets everything for the best. He is never mean or little in his disputes, never takes unfair

advantage, never mistakes personalities or sharp sayings for arguments, or insinuates evil which he dare not say out.... He has too much good sense to be affronted at insults, he is too well employed to remember injuries.... He knows the weakness of human reason as well as its strength, its province, and its limits.... He respects piety and devotion; he even supports institutions as venerable, beautiful or useful to which he does not assent....

In quite a different idiom, but with identical concern, the sensitive American novelist, Edward Lewis Wallant, has one of his perceptive characters observe:

... what a little thing (the hurting of one's soul) was in that neighborhood—one person's little humiliation; it was less than nothing there. People torment each other worse ways, much worse. With poor people, it shows more, they actually do physical crimes. More civilized people can do to each other more refined, without lifting a hand.

Clearly, we need trained intelligence and we need political skill, but far more than either we need a reaffirming of our basic faith in, and love for, our common humanity, not as an abstract principle, or used in bludgeoning confrontation, but expressed by each of us in the living witness of the individual encounters of our works and days. Whatever our private hope of heaven, mindful of how fragile and transient human life is, we know, with Sir Thomas Browne, that "it cannot be long before we lie down in darkness, and have our light in ashes."

Aldous Huxley, whose death on November 22, 1963 was obscured by President Kennedy's death that same day, wrote in a moving letter to his wife: "I would like to feel that I can love you with so much understanding tenderness that I shall always know what to do, or what to refrain from doing in order to help you in your strength and support you in your vulnerability...."

If the transposition is not too forced—and Huxley in his later years, I believe, would not have thought so—*this* is the kind of concern we will have for each other if our education, to this point and throughout the remainder of our lives, takes proper root.

Mr. Chancellor, it is with profound pleasure and affection for this class that I present the graduates of 1969 for the conferring of degrees.

Remarks
Fourth Annual
Commencement Exercises

Northside Hall Auditorium, June 3, 1970

The past year has been a time of great losses for the nation, but IUSB's graduates, in particular the first master's degree graduates, have learned and will continue to learn "with the desire to be not movers and shakers, but, rather, stewards and servants of the talents given to us . . . ."

President Sutton, Vice-President Ryan, Mr. Lucas, graduating students, ladies and gentlemen:

If, as one of Shakespeare's sage characters observed, there are tongues in brooks, sermons in stones, and good in everything, maybe we can extract from the chill and rainy visage of this day a final lesson for the Class of 1970 as it is here convened in what will always remain its climactic formal gathering. I will try to avoid clichés about clouds with silver linings or the night being darkest just before the dawn, but I would like to offer a few thoughts about the seeming paradox created by the aspiring hopes traditionally expressed at happy ceremonies such as this when those same hopes are measured against the dismaying truth that year after year after year we point to the staggering human problems which yet await solution.

The problems are almost ritualistically familiar: war and peace; equity and justice; religious, racial, and political disharmony; physical and psychic well-being—maybe, in essence, the single problem of bridging the salt, estranging sea which divides us one from the other and from the rich possibilities of our best selves.

And yet, if there was no paradox and no ambiguity in the managing and understanding of human affairs, there would be no need for humane learning, and no need for schools which—whatever their current imperfections—best advance that learning. The past academic year has produced still further evidence that what has been ignored in mindless attempts to preserve a past that never was or never should have been, and what has been ignored in mindless attempts to destroy a past (and a present) that has been selectively defined, alike constitute the gravest enemy to the truly liberating purpose of education, a purpose which will always be sensitive not only to the distances yet to go but to the road already come.

More than that, the humble spirit of liberating education will, I think, be skeptical of claims that in this, our worldly life, there have been, or can be, paradises or Utopias of either the past or the future. Maybe, on reflection, road or river metaphors for the progress made by a civilization or an individual life are not really very apt, and what we need, rather, are more evolutionary or biological images: to think, for example, of each part or phase of our imperfect understanding as a kind of node or chrysalis which—if all goes well—will branch or spring forth into ever clearer understanding, not only of intellectual matters but of moral and aesthetic matters as well.

Learning, pursued not arrogantly or in fierce competition, but in a spirit of wise passiveness and with the desire to be not movers and shakers but, rather, stewards and servants of the talents given to us— such learning, I think, gives the best assurance we can get that all will go well. The precision of thought, feeling, and language engendered by such learning should make it possible for us to know again that not only sticks and stones can break our bones, but that words do in fact hurt us, and can hurt us grievously. Rancor, and rancorous language, whatever the source and however pure the actual or alleged motive, always clouds reason, and must, therefore, always be alien to the work the university and all civilized institutions will most properly be doing.

The great English poet, John Keats, in looking for fresh ways to proclaim his wonder, astonishment, and praise for the beautiful things that move the human heart once wrote: "I want a fairer word than fair." An equivalent of looking for the fairer word is for educated men and women to know that we need not give up using familiar words by default to those who use them for their own oppressive ends. As educated people, can we not find it possible to hear phrases like "law and order" without grimacing in the knowledge that such phrases have all too frequently been used by charlatans and demagogues? Can we not believe, or come to believe, that one idea behind civil and church law, no matter how discriminatorily such law has been applied or formulated, is that there is an inherent, natural, and organic principle of order in our human and divinely mysterious universe which we must seek in humility, and revere even when we find it embodied imperfectly—as it always will be—in the evolving institutions of our fragile civilization? Have we not learned that anarchy and chaos are the enemy of that civilization even as a brutally mechanical notion of externally imposed order is an enemy?

And now, speaking for the faculty and the administration of Indiana University at South Bend, but speaking also in my personal voice as well, I hope your experience at IUSB—all things considered—has been as fully satisfying to you as it has been to us who have had the high privilege of serving you. Today all of you—and, in particular, our first masters degree graduates—join the nearly 700 Indiana University students who have graduated from this campus since our first small class of 30 graduated only three years ago. You constitute more than half the total of that near-700, and in years to come will be joined by thousands and tens of thousands more who we know will give, with you, living witness of loyalty and devotion to the distinguished university which deserves our deepest affection.

Mr. President, I take great pleasure in presenting to you the Class of 1970 for the conferring of degrees.

May 6, 1970. Lester Wolfson breaks ground for the Northside west addition. On the left is South Bend Mayor Lloyd Allen. Anti-Vietnam War demonstrators can be seen in the background.

Wolfson-Nixon Letters
May 5, 1970 and June 24, 1970

*News stories of secret U.S. B-52 bombings of targets in neutral Cambodia
where North Vietnam's military had established base sanctuaries intensified
anti-Vietnam War protest across the U.S., and on May 4, 1970, National
Guard troops killed four students during a protest at Kent State University.
The following day, Chancellor Wolfson sent a letter of protest to President Nixon, who replied on June 24. The bombings continued until Congress voted to
terminate them on August 14, 1973.*

May 5, 1970

The Honorable Richard M. Nixon
The White House
1600 Pennsylvania Avenue, N.W.
Washington, D.C.

Dear President Nixon:

I write to express my deep dismay at the extension of the war to
Cambodia, and urge you to re-consider immediately both the need for,
and the dire consequences of, such an action.

I grieve too at the deaths of the students at Kent State University.
While the causes of violence are many and complex, certainly one cause
over which you can exercise considerable control is the inflammatory
language used by high public officials in their comments on the crises of
our time.

Yours truly,

Lester M. Wolfson
Chancellor

LMW:rm

Gloria Kaufman speaks at anti-Vietnam War
teach-in and rally at IU South Bend

Vietnam Veterans protest the war

Dr. Lester M. Wolfson
Chancellor
Indiana University at South Bend
1825 Northside Boulevard
South Bend, Indiana 46615

THE WHITE HOUSE

THE WHITE HOUSE

WASHINGTON

June 24, 1970

Dear Dr. Wolfson:

Your recent message expresses the deep concern
which all of us must feel toward the challenges
facing our country. The recent deaths at Kent
State University and elsewhere have gravely
saddened the nation. No violence is justifiable,
and I am determined that we will find methods of
dealing with violence which would not endanger
the lives of innocent people.

Contrary to an impression many have received, the
Cambodia mission does not represent an expansion
of the war in Vietnam. I made the decision to
undertake this action for the very reasons that
the dissidents are demonstrating: to end the
war sooner. The protests concern me because I
know how deeply these young people feel, but I
know also that what I have done will accomplish
the goals they want.

In my May 8 press conference, I commented that it
is advisable when the action is hot to keep the
rhetoric cool. This is not to say that dissent
should be stifled. I have for years defended
the right of dissent, but I have always opposed
the use of violence. On university campuses the
rule of reason should prevail over the rule of
force and I hope that in the weeks and months

2

ahead we can develop better lines of communication to the student generation and also to school
administrators.

With my best wishes,

Sincerely,

Richard Nixon

Dr. Lester M. Wolfson
Chancellor
Indiana University at South Bend
1825 Northside Boulevard
South Bend, Indiana 46615

IUSB in the '70s
Delivered at the Fall Faculty Meeting,
September 26, 1970

*The campus should celebrate enrollment growth, as well as the current construc-
tion of Northside West. It should also face the current problems in university
institutional life—incivility and disrespect for the values of the informed heart
and mind. Ignorance and indiscretion endanger the delicate, quasi-aristocratic
academic community. We must formulate our own code of ethics.*

This is, for me, the seventh September (with the days dwin-
dling down) that I have been given a spot of time to say some
things I hope you want to hear. In the past, I have entitled
these annual papers "Remarks," or—using the old ceremonial crutch—
"The State of the South Bend Campus." Neither label seems very
appropriate to me this year. "Remarks" is too casual, and "The State of
. . ." too conventionally mannered to convey my sense of the urgency
of the current problems in university institutional life. I immodestly
wish that by speaking of "IUSB in the '70s" I can take the long view
appropriate to the beginning of a new decade—not to mention, on
a more sidereal scale, the dawning of the Age of Aquarius. But I am
sobered by the notion that, in the long run, only short views may be
possible, and ponder also the fate of Tiresias, doomed to Dante's Hell
with head forever twisted backward, because he thought he could foretell the future.

Nonetheless, some things which were foretold have come to pass.
If you need assurance, look out the windows of the gallery hall on the
second floor of Northside to see the concrete columns—our Pelion on

Ossa—reaching to the sky of our spatial need. When that structure is completed in a year and a half or so, we will have gained room nearly equal to Northside, Greenlawn, and Riverside combined. Among other capital items, we are asking the 1971 General Assembly for a direct appropriation to build a free-standing library, and bonding authority to build a Student Union. All of this is in keeping with an effort to stay up with expanding enrollments and to realize in an evenly graduated way an excellent space norm over a series of four or five biennia. In addition, what we had projected in 1966 for program development to be achieved by 1975 will almost certainly be reached by that time, if not sooner. Our 30 graduates in our first class of 1967 had grown to some 370 in our class of 1970. Master's degree programs have been established in elementary education, in business, and in special education. We have embarked on a number of allied medical and dental curricula, and through extra-mural grants are currently offering programs which reach persons who ordinarily would not, or could not, come to college.

From 1964 to 1970, enrollment has increased from 2,000 to 4,800; hours taken from 14,000 to over 45,000; the full-time professional staff from 25 to 125; the annual operating budget (exclusive of auxiliary enterprises, extra-mural funding, and operating support from the central University system) from under $600,000 to nearly $3,000,000. Put another way, in a six year period advances show enrollment is nearly 2 1/2 times as large; hours taken more than tripled; full-time appointments quintupled; and operating budget quintupled.

South Bend continues to be the most rapidly growing Indiana University campus. Both total students and hours taken are up approximately 20% from last fall. In September, 1969 we enrolled some 4,000 students; this fall, about 4,800. Next fall the figure will be well over 5,000.

The administrative de-centralization of the University first begun in July, 1968, has continued apace. Earlier this month, Dr. Walt P. Risler's administrative title was changed by the Trustees from "Associate Dean" to "Dean of Faculties"; Dr. Albert J. Beutler's title was changed from "Assistant Dean" to "Dean of Student Services"; Eugene E. Love's title was changed from "Assistant to the Dean of the University Division" (the Dean being in Bloomington) to "Director of the

University Division." Although a year ago we had informally dropped the practice of referring to our local Assistant Chairmen as "Assistant," the Trustees have now made "Chairman" the official title of our departmental heads, and I foresee (with no special divination) that in the fullness of the time Academic Divisional Chairmen will be styled "Dean."

All of these new titles merely in themselves may not signify as much as they will a few years hence, but they are both timely and richly deserved by the men to whom they have been given. Besides, semanticists notwithstanding, to English-speaking peoples a rose by any other name does *not* smell as sweet, and Adam was surely right when he named the hippopotamus as he did because it *looked* like a hippopotamus.

I will not say more at the moment about the present still-fluid structure of the seven-campus system which is Indiana University, or of the five-campus sub-system of which South Bend is part. Nor will I say more about the still-evolving responsibilities of the various offices within that system. Instead, over the next few months, in the weekly *Newsletter* we place in the mail each Wednesday, we will include items which should be particularly helpful in orienting the new colleagues we especially welcome today. I trust that for now enough has been said to suggest that signs of health and growth abound, most of it directly attributable to the many good people who have served this campus well through a happy blend of talent and commitment.

But there is a beast that lurks in the jungle, and it is not the subtly rarefied beast of quivering sensibility which marks the characters of Henry James's fiction. This animal is far more gross, and unless contained could well devour not only all the hopes we have for better teaching, learning, and service at IUSB in the '70s, but could quell the great civilizing force which nearly all colleges and universities have exerted on so much that is predatory in society at large. That beast, coming out ever more frequently into open territory, can be named as the fundamental disrespect for, and suspicion of, the informed heart and mind which it has been the university's job to create when it is going about its most central business. Perhaps in some dim way our society has valued the intellectual virtues—particularly if it could be satisfied that certain restrictively defined notions of good decorum, good citizenship, and good economic acumen were getting primary emphasis in our schools and colleges. But when the university—sometimes even in its implicit (and inevitable) role as critic, rather than in its equally implicit (and inevitable) role as celebrator, of the status quo—exacerbates the public patience too greatly, you see how many figs are given for the disinterested search for truth or for the refinement of aesthetic awareness.

If, like Socrates, one is willing to grant that most—if not all—of those who condemn the innocent do so out of ignorance rather than out of malice, and if one believes in the liberating power of knowledge, how incredible that, through indiscretion at the very least, many persons in the academic community have endangered the delicate kind of quasi-aristocratic institution the university is, an institution which, in its deepest values, exists all too often by sufferance when we should wish it to flourish through being loved. Need I say that I am not holding out any brief for rednecks, those implacable and inflexible writers of hate-letters who relentlessly scavenge for imagined treason and immorality. But surely we have something to answer for whenever we temporize with anyone—students, or colleagues, or the public at large—about the fundamental values of personal courtesy, open discourse, and rational progression in argument.

Saul Bellow's observant Artur Sammler says,

> . . . it is sometimes necessary to repeat what all know. All map makers should place the Mississippi in the same location, and avoid originality. It may be boring, but one has to know where he is. We cannot have the Mississippi flowing toward the Rockies for a change.

Anything we can do at IUSB in the 1970s, or which can be done in all but the most secluded colleges anywhere, will depend on our willingness to be boring, to know where we are, to repeat the old verities: that for a faculty, in particular, college is a place for careful thought, for wide—sometimes brooding—speculation, for painstaking attention to the logic, art, and craft of the learned disciplines and professions. It is not a place for partisan political action, which can only make it vulnerable to any power and mood of external political fortune. It is not a place for idiosyncratic practices which purport to heal the allegedly ailing young by therapeutic grading systems; nor is it a place for garrulous camaraderie with the young, whether occasioned by a search for disciples, or a search for one's own lost or vanishing youth. Least of all is it a place for the distorting of academic freedom to mean one is free to do as he pleases with his classes—including not meeting them at all on any discernible schedule.

I do not say these things as a kind of blanket innuendo which implies all are guilty—even if you grant that I have listed true offenses. There is too much of that kind of thing abroad in the land, creating so much suspicion and division that it gets harder and harder to appreciate the jest which goes: "Just because I'm paranoid doesn't mean that I don't *really* have enemies." I say these things in part because we are increasingly being held to account by a public which is, to say the least, no longer benignly indifferent to what we do, but more importantly because I think that by a kind of collective erosion some of us are not working as hard as we might be, or perhaps (more accurately) that in an old theological notion of sloth, although we may be frenetically active, we are not giving enough time to our proper devotions. If *that* is true, we should be our own toughest critics.

It is not "Catch-22" but "Cliché-22" to say that unless we formulate our own code of ethics, unless we set down more formally what we long thought we had informally taken for granted, people will not be wanting who will attempt to make one for us. As many of you know, in IU an all-University Committee has already presented a preliminary code to the University Faculty Council, and a refined version will be considered soon. Deans, chairmen, and faculty members at UCLA have recently received communications from Chancellor Charles Young enjoining them to develop codes and procedures that will bring whatever consensus may be possible to diverse temperaments. The administration will ultimately be responsible for enforcing whatever codes are adopted.

While we should—and undoubtedly will—be alert to any code nuances which threaten due process or genuine freedom, I hope that we can save energy by moderating the kind of contentiousness which Shakespeare's Mercutio found in Tybalt, who quarreled with a man whose cough in the street had awakened Tybalt's dog as it lay asleep in the sun.

In looking back on my comments, I see that I have not really said very much about IUSB in the 1970s. But as with the making of books, with the making of colleges there is no end. New ones are created, existing ones grow and change. This year we celebrate IU's sesquicentennial, since the legislation creating Indiana University was passed on January 20, 1820. But it was about 1900 before IU, Bloomington had 1,000 students. I graduated from Michigan in 1945, and only recently learned that Michigan had graduated its first class exactly 100 years before (in 1845) although 1817 is set as its year of birth. If we plan too tightly, we may limit our choices—to take on a program in special education, for example. If we plan too loosely, we may become the prey of an energetic department, a department afflicted with hubris—in William Arrowsmith's analysis, something which is, and ought to be, a garden, aspiring to be a jungle.

What I have been implying is that the national mood will have much to do with the shape and scope of what we will be able to offer in the 1970's. Indiana as a state and as a university has so far been spared much of the acrimony which has seriously weakened public confidence in higher education in several other states. Indiana University at all of its campuses has been blessed with responsible students and faculty members, but deep cracks and stresses form and reform. Fanatics exude a malign nimbus which envelopes the unstable and unwary. Now is the time for people in universities to be as wise as serpents and innocent as doves, a time for spiritual continence and restraint. There may be reason to agree with wise old Sammler once again when he reflects that

> the worst enemies of civilization might . . . prove to be its petted intellectuals who attacked it at its weakest moments —attacked it in the name of proletarian revolution, in the name of reason, and in the name of irrationality, in the name of visceral depth, in the name of sex, in the name of perfect instantaneous freedom. For what it amounted to was limitless demand—insatiability, refusal of the doomed creature (death being sure and final) to go away from this earth unsatisfied. A

full bill of demand and complaint was therefore presented by each individual. Non-negotiable. Recognizing no scarcity of supply in any human department. Enlightenment? Marvelous! But out of hand, wasn't it?

I think our task as academic men and women in the years immediately ahead is to get matters back in hand, to be modest about what we can do institutionally to solve social problems directly, but to be more un-apologetically convinced than ever before that what we can do, by means of our scholarly disciplines, to help our students see more clearly and feel more exactly will have its sure effects in the betterment of life.

Most cordial welcome to all. I look forward to a good year.

Lester Wolfson with John W. Ryan, IU President, at
1971 IU South Bend Commencement

By 1971 commencement exercises had outgrown Northside auditorium. Left: Graduates, families and friends convene at the Morris Civic Auditorium in downtown South Bend. Below: Faculty assembles for the procession.

Sufficient Unto the Day, or Whither IUSB?

Delivered at the Fall Faculty Meeting, August 26, 1972

While we reckon with society's increasing distrust of the traditional college curriculum, we continue to explore the possibilities for redefinition of the curriculum across the margins of the established disciplines. Does the current curriculum have intrinsic human importance, vocational applicability, and social usefulness? We must affirm our institutional responsibility for critical awareness, investigative power, and aesthetic sensibility.

Every fall, as I seek to say something that may merit your attention, I am tempted to the easy way out taken by one of my boyhood friends. Believing in the need to stay in human touch, and yet recognizing the extreme difficulty of doing so, he writes me a letter each year—by all the usual criteria a letter absolutely non-communicative, but withal a beautiful model of impeccable form. Invariably, with proper spacing, it goes: Salutation, Body, Complimentary Close. Such a letter takes no risks, least of all the risk of being misunderstood, or of striking a pose which can be excused only in artists or gifted madmen. Thus, an Emily Dickinson can say: "This is my letter to the World/That never wrote to Me . . . ," or an inward-turning, super-intellectual, like Saul Bellow's Moses Herzog, can write notes to God: "How my mind has struggled to make coherent sense. I have not been too good at it. But have desired to do your unknowable will,

taking it, and you, without symbols. Everything of intensest significance. Especially if divested of me."

Yet, finally, the temptation to take my friend's safe way by saying nothing must be resisted, since the beginning of a new academic
year almost demands that someone attempt to survey what is real,
and what only imagined, in our institutional condition; to rehearse
accomplishments, catalogue disappointments, and project hopes. I
am pleased to have this ninth opportunity to make that effort at
assessment: I begin, as customary, with a few measures of quantitative growth. I do so with some slight trepidation since I know that
there is understandable, if at the last unwarranted, concern that we
may be playing a numbers game. I am as dismayed as any one that
by far the most frequent question I get in the community at large is,
"How many students do you have now?" I hasten to add, however,
that the question often follows praise for the powerful resource and
reservoir that IUSB has become, and is becoming, for the total cultural good of north-central Indiana.

With no more verbal moues, then, let me come right at these
quantitative measures. In the eight years since 1964, IUSB enrollment
has grown from 2,000 to over 5,000; the full-time professional staff
from 24 to nearly 170; the operating budget from under $500,000
to about $5,000,000. Put another way, enrollment is more than 2
1/2 times higher, the full-time staff has grown seven-fold, and the
annual budget ten-fold. A final comparison might note that the 1972
graduating class of 710 was almost 24 times as large as the first class
of 30 in 1967.

And now, having recited such figures, I suspect that there is probably no need ever to do so again, since it now seems impossible for
anyone to deny the fact of our substantial presence, our viability, and
our readiness to assume the essential self-determination that will
have come to us within the Indiana University system by 1975. In
the past four years we have been moving steadily toward the goal
of operational autonomy announced in 1968 by President Stahr,
forwarded by President Sutton, and now given great impetus by
President Ryan and Chancellor Bowman. Moreover, we are at last
beginning to develop the physical facilities—both on scene and in

the offing—that will better enable us to do our appointed tasks. I will say more about that matter in other contexts as the year progresses.

I intended something of a homonymic pun in part of the announced title of these remarks, "Whither IUSB?" for although a future for our campus is surely assured, you cannot have missed any more than I have that the *shape* of that future, as indeed the future of all higher education, is less certainly predictable than it was as recently as a year ago. A spate of articles and sponsored reports over the past year has questioned with growing fervor the intrinsic human importance, the vocational applicability, and the social usefulness of the traditional college curriculum, fragmented and option-laden as that curriculum has become. This general suspicion and skepticism is compounded when professional academicians, such as economist Fritz Machlup, sharpen and define anew distinctions between three types of instruction offered in most colleges today: thinner, broader, and genuinely higher education. "Thinner" refers to remedial training; "broader" to those acculturating courses taken up in college because of lack of time or opportunity in high school; and "higher" education, accessible by intellect and motivation to perhaps not more than five or ten per cent of the population, to those studies which build sequentially, cumulatively, and profoundly on the principles lying at the heart of any coherent discipline. While Machlup finds value in all three types of offering, there can be little doubt that the growing discontinuity between present curricula and available jobs, coupled with what many see as the incompatibility of missions within a single institution, will affect the level of both financial and moral support unless we can unitedly become more persuasive advocates for the subjects we hold dear. I urge that each of you begin to formulate the best justification you can, since in about a month we will have an opportunity to react to the preliminary draft of a long-range plan for post high-school education in Indiana currently being developed by the Commission for Higher Education. Just how much "higher education" in Machlup's sense will be supported is difficult to foretell but I hope, and believe, that this faculty will make a most generous estimate of both the indispensable need for such support and the capability of more students to benefit from genuine higher studies than Machlup's academic conservatism will allow.

We already have much of the preliminary work done for an apologia, since in response to Chancellor Bowman's request and mine each department and division last year prepared a statement of mission, while a faculty and student Priorities Committee, under the valorous direction of Chairman John Peck and Co-Chairman Wayne Krepel, produced an impressive document which I have publicly thanked them for last spring, and here do so again. Shortly, that complete report will be distributed in its entirety, exactly as written, to every full-time faculty member. As a sneak preview, let me say that the Committee, with noble impartiality, looked upon all the efforts we are currently making, found them good, and worthy of retention. That judgment may prove a little worrisome, since Jacques Barzun once told how the Columbia University administration had pledged its support in seeking funds to help the academic divisions to reach their level of desired excellence if the divisions, in turn, would relentlessly scrutinize their present expenses to see which, if any, could be eliminated. While I do not remember the exact result, when the ledger was balanced the magnitude of difference was something on the order of $40,000,000 needed and $400,000 (or was it $40,000?) possible to be saved. But away with these pestilential vapors!

Still—are great sums required before there can be the energetic dialogue of mind which is the living witness that liberating education has occurred, and is occurring? Despite the excesses of futurists like Alvin Toffler, Wordsworth more than 170 years ago, and John Ciardi only last week may well have said all that needs saying about a curriculum which will, finally, get the admiration and support it needs. As an endorsement for all the arts, as well as the sciences, Wordsworth spoke of the poet as the

> rock of defense for human nature; an upholder and preserver, carrying everywhere with him relationship and love. In spite of differences of soil and climate, of language and manners, of laws and customs, in spite of things silently gone out of mind, and things violently destroyed; the poet binds together by passion and knowledge the vast empire of human society, as it is spread over the whole earth, and over all time.... The remotest discoveries of the chemist, the botanist, or mineralogist, will

be as proper objects of the poet's art as any upon which it can be employed, if the time should ever come when these things shall be familiar to us, and the relations under which they are contemplated by the followers of these respective sciences shall be manifestly and palpably material to us as enjoying and suffering beings.

Ciardi, in praise of E. B. White, who I would guess is known to some of your children through *Charlotte's Web*, said of him: "When he came on to the world's data, it was never his thought to reduce them to mere clicks for teletype transmission. He felt what he came across in the world and reported how it felt. And the good reader's reaction was always, 'Yes. That is how a thoughtful and sensitive man with a gift for words, a long human memory, and the grace of a generous mind must feel about these things.'"

To bring some of these implications for curriculum and institutional purpose closer to home, some of you will recall that in an exuberant moment last year, I allowed myself to say:

> ... the only two disciplines which any college should concern itself with are music and mathematics. "Music" is used metaphorically to stand for all the organizable instruction directed to man's expressive, affective, aesthetic dimension; and "mathematics" is used metaphorically to stand for all the organizable instruction directed to man's cerebral, ratiocinative, analytical powers which stand at the root of all significant science. In between these poles just about everything that deserves intellectual or aesthetic effort would fall.

One of our colleagues in mathematics made a written response to that statement. I want to share it with you now. He wrote:

> ... I would like to comment very briefly on your identification of mathematics and music as polar opposites of curriculum construction. Speaking as a mathematician, I believe that mathematics is a kind of abstract music, and that music is a special kind of mathematics. Therefore, I identify your polar

opposites so closely together that they rush into a merger which leaves no room for anything in between. To me, the thing that gets left out most here is history. This seems a pity, especially at IUSB where the historians seem like such nice guys and bright minds.

In my opinion, the true polar opposites of curriculum construction are on the one hand, love of the pure Platonic forms in which mathematicians and musicians can totally immerse themselves, and on the other hand, the attempt to make these formal structures 'relevant' to the concrete, mucky, sweaty, brutal, and terrifying realities of human existence. The attempt to find in such Platonic forms as TRUTH, JUSTICE, LOVE, HONOR a meaning for actual human life is one which must be made by the "humanistic" disciplines, such as history, and your own discipline, literature. In my own case, I decided early to flee the murky complexities of such an attempt and settle for the bright, clear inhuman world of pure form.

That colleague and I have not started any pen-pal correspondence but I did answer him in this way:

I am . . . grateful for your thoughtful and illuminating comments about the music-mathematics dichotomy. I fully accept your analysis as at least as valid as anything in my own. I suppose where historians demonstrate a true sense of the joys and terrors in the human scene as viewed by historians they are with the "musicians." When historians catalogue, summarize, classify, infer, etc. (all this in the best sense of those words) I would place them with the "mathematicians." But, finally, as you suggest, the two concepts may after all be really only one.

. . . as I consider the daily mucky aspects of my own job, it is very heartening to be reminded by a letter such as yours that there is an intellectual ideal we are trying to serve here. We must find opportunities to discuss these matters further.

I regret that I did not exert myself more to find those opportunities, and suggest now that maybe the Committee on Teaching might want to follow up on last year's fine panels on teaching approaches by inviting students and the rest of us to programs in 1972-73 that will explain and defend the rationale for including various studies in our curriculum. Are there not root principles that can be defined, explicated, and ramified in such a way that we do not fall into the trap of endless course and program proliferation?

This question leads me to wonder if through occasional self-indulgence, we ourselves may have contributed to these parlous times for true higher education. Assailed on the one side by partisans of restrictive vocationalism and professionalism, and on the other by those who wish college to provide almost any experience except intellectual discipline, there is a chance that the university as a place for disinterested contemplation, fresh discovery, play of mind, respect for evidence, and compassionate social concern may be seen as increasingly anachronistic. To prevent that danger, we have been rightly charged to plan more carefully, and to render more exact account of our activities. We must, and should, respond to such a charge, not defensively but seeing in it a marvelous chance to blazon forth our conviction that what we do in developing critical awareness, investigative power, and aesthetic sensitivity demands a proportionate investment of our state's, and our nation's, resources.

Despite some legitimate cause for concern, we stand on the brink of greater institutional freedom and responsibility than we have ever known before. Many good men and women, both here and afar, have labored to bring us to this happy point in our history. At the risk of special pleading, I believe that IUSB is in many ways the strongest of the smaller Indiana University campuses. Although we still have much yet to do, no other regional campus matches us in the size and quality of our programs in the arts—music, theatre, communications, writing, painting, and sculpture. We have given more attention to philosophy and to physics than our sister campuses have given. We have steadily growing strength in mathematics, chemistry, biology, and are at last beginning a program in earth sciences. Many of our faculty in history, English, and political science have already accomplished distinguished work. The developing programs in psychology and sociology have attracted many of our very best students. With the reinstatement of credit for beginning language studies, and with burgeoning international interest, I hope that we will soon see flourishing in our foreign language program.

Equal praise must go to our programs in Education, and in Business and Economics. Among other strengths, Education has worked in fruitful partnership with local schools in a way unequalled anywhere in the state. The fertile and persistent efforts of the Business and Economics faculty have been recognized in South Bend and in the state in many ways. Studies in taxation and finance have been used as basic legislative documents, and the St. Joseph Bank has just pledged to underwrite the cost of publishing the Division's Economic Indicators Bulletin. Students in our young paramedical and paradental programs uniformly distinguish themselves on national tests, etc. We anticipate critically important work to be done in our new program in public and environmental affairs under the directorship of Tom DeCoster, and a re-vitalizing of the entire continuing education thrust under Helen Archibald's leadership.

While we follow both internal and external mandates to plan for the future, in a deep, philosophical sense we can be aware that much of our planning is already done. For in the commitment we have already made to our chosen careers, we know that for those who have faith in the ideal of human knowledge, just as for those who have a profounder faith, there is no real need to take thought for the morrow; for the morrow shall take thought for the things of itself. Sufficient unto the day is the evil thereof.

Warmest and most heartfelt welcome to all, and so as to take no further risks, let me emulate my friend by adding only, "Complimentary Close."

The Penetralium of Mystery
Delivered at the Fall Faculty Meeting,
August 25, 1973

Illuminated by the Keatsian principle of Negative Capability, IUSB's distrust of the uncertainties inherent in state-wide budget negotiations and appropriations should not disable its diligent efforts to secure adequate and appropriate state funding for its programs and campus growth.

Our first meeting of the fall is rather ceremonial, but the old-timers (i.e., anyone who has been here at least two years) will recognize that the Senate is truly in session when I tell them that I have already been chided on the allegedly incorrect form of the word "penetralium" in the title of these remarks. While the linguistically insecure might agonize over whether one says "ice tea" or "iced tea," it has been suggested by Dean Peyser that the word I intended should have been "penetralia" or perhaps "penetralis." He clearly will be a welcome addition to that mixture of lyceum, Chautauqua, forum, hustings, semantic castle, and training ground for stand-up comedians otherwise known as the IUSB Academic Senate. But like the man who gets caught when he sooner or later tries a White Owl, anyone who challenges "penetralium" must reckon with a peachily unimpeachable master of the English language—the poet John Keats.

Writing to his brothers on Sunday, December 21, 1817, Keats's rare intelligence and ranging wisdom is in good evidence when he says:

> I had not a dispute but a disquisition, with Dilke on various subjects; several things dove-tailed in my mind, and at once it struck me what quality went to form a Man of Achievement,

especially in Literature, and which Shakespeare possessed so enormously—I mean *Negative Capability*, that is, when a man is capable of being in uncertainties, mysteries, doubts without any irritable reaching after fact and reason—Coleridge, for instance, would let go by a fine isolated verisimilitude caught from the Penetralium of mystery, from being incapable of remaining content with half-knowledge.

Well, whether it is "penetralium" or "penetralia," the word refers to inner parts or recesses, and when Keats writes of the "penetralium of mystery," he is talking about the unfathomable depths of final reality, a reality which for him is glimpsed primarily through the hints and guesses provided by the silent workings of great art. All of Keats's speculations on these matters in his short life culminate in the affirmation—profession of faith, rather—at the end of the "Ode on a Grecian Urn" that beauty is truth, truth beauty. Coleridge's fault, as Keats saw it, was that he would too often obscure the value of his aesthetic vision by murky philosophizing which attempted to fix, catalogue, define, or explain absolutely those things knowable, and then only partially, through artistic insight or the loving immediacy of human interaction. "Fact" and "reason," in one sense our stock-in-trade in colleges and universities, can be, as Keats thought they were for Coleridge, snares and delusions if we conclude that through even the most comprehensive gathering of information, or the most resourceful application of method and analysis, we can finally catch everything knowable, or most needful to know, about personality, character, destiny, motive, and act.

I hope it will not be some monumental non sequitur or trivializing as I now apply Keats's grand assessment to three of our specific concerns at IUSB—concerns having important implications for the kind of institution we are, and are to be. I want to suggest—implicitly for the most part—that as we continue to work at those concerns with all the proper energy we can muster, we not dissipate strength for professional effort by "irritable reaching after fact and reason...from being incapable of remaining content with half-knowledge."

The first concern is the 1973-74 budget, and the prospects for 1974-75. I speak here not of the near-universal inclination to feel that there is never enough to go around. Juliet can say to Romeo, "My bounty is as boundless as the sea,/My love as deep; the more I give to thee,/The more I have, for both are infinite." But the state's resources are neither boundless nor infinite, and one should be able to sympathize at least partially with Governor Bowen's statement that new governmental appropriations have gone up by 9% and expenditures for higher education by 12%. Just as the Governor has said that the universities will have to reach their own conclusions as to whether or not, all things considered, they have been treated fairly, I suppose each of us has to decide whether we collectively, through reason and persuasive skill, have made the best case possible, or perhaps simply conclude with the T.V. Tarzan in the beer ad, "There's a jungle out there," and we've just had a hard day.

But, as indicated, it is not to this that I wish to speak, but rather to the vexing question of what is happening internally to the IUSB share of the total Indiana University budget. It is here, I think, that half-knowledge has made us more restive than we need be. Let me tell you all that I know about this issue, which has already prompted Senate resolutions and questions addressed to Chancellor Bowman and to our area legislators.

When President Ryan first became Vice-President and Chancellor for Regional Campuses some five years ago, one of his first acts was to press for equal funding for equivalent programs on all Indiana University campuses. That effort has been sustained by him and by Chancellor Bowman, and indeed has been formalized by recommendations of the Indiana Commission for Higher Education. More than that, IU officers have been constantly vigilant about the apparently more favorable funding given to other state institutions—notably Purdue. The disparities, as is usual in such cases, resulted from historical accident, political pressure, and perhaps some nodding inattentiveness in the past. Those circumstances are far less apt to be controlling in the future, as careful planning at all levels becomes the order of the day.

Again, some five years ago, when the University was reorganized into three major units—Bloomington, Indianapolis, and Regional Campus Administration—funds were appropriated to each of the three units, with RCA being charged with further sub-dividing its appropriation among the various regional campuses, as well as maintaining necessary funds for its own central operations. This year, for the first time, the General Assembly has made a separate line-item appropriation for each of the eight campuses, and while there has been some disagreement within the University as to whether that is the best way to go, it appears now that the pattern for the future has been set, a pattern which is compatible with the scheduled phasing out of Regional Campus Administration in the near future.

With the increasing operational authority and responsibility which is devolving to each campus, individual budgets now reflect more immediately exact operational costs, costs which are mainly provided for by the state appropriation plus projected income from student fees (some 6.5 million dollars gross for IUSB in 1973-74).

As most of you know, the appropriation for IUSB for this biennium is both absolutely and relatively considerably higher than it is for our sister campuses in the regional campus system. The bone of contention within the University is whether or not the appropriations actually reflect legislative intent, or resulted from an error in that a formula figure was applied to an incorrect base. Whatever the final determination is, the practical effect for 1973-74 is that the University as a whole has had tremendous difficulty in coming up with workable budgets for several of its campuses, and has had to avail itself of every legal and tactical option to work out partial solutions. One result of that effort is that currently IUSB is being charged a higher service cost than would ordinarily be the case, but the extra cost is still less than half the "excess" appropriation if, in fact, an error has been made. The University a few weeks ago *did* claim error, and requested re-allocation of funds among the various regional campuses. If the request is granted, our appropriation for 1974-75 will be less than the figure currently set for this year, with implications which I stand ready to discuss with appropriate faculty groups throughout the year.

I know there are tangles in this thicket where I have barely touched, but if we can manage some of the negative capability which Keats found so admirable in Shakespeare, whatever minimal glimpses we have had of the integrity of an institution like Indiana University should suggest caution in reaching unhappy conclusions about its way of wrestling with this particular problem. Unless life, individual or corporate, is nothing but a raw power struggle—and what reasonable man or woman believes so?—how will we have gained if temporary advantage leads to one's being clobbered next week, or next year, or the year after that?

The word "communication" is much over-worked, and particularly wearing to anyone who has learned that it too often means not "you haven't told me anything," but "you haven't told me what I wanted to hear." Yet I would guess that in this matter of the budget communication has not been as good as it might have been. We will work locally at improvement, and I am confident that other IU officers have the same intention.

Before turning to the second of the three matters I wish to comment on—and staying with communication for a minute—let me state that at the second of two meetings I had last year with chairpersons of Academic Senate committees, we agreed that a quarterly written statement on the status of various projects and conditions would be useful. The first of such statements will appear in mid-September.

About the second concern I shall be quite brief, since the third one is a special instance of the second and I will wish to treat it at somewhat greater length.

In my remarks last year, I referred to the Report on Priorities, prepared during 1971-72 by a committee chaired by John Peck, and co-chaired by Wayne Krepel. That Report was distributed in September to the full-time staff, and I had asked that its recommendations be a matter of Academic Senate consideration. I cannot recall, nor do the minutes reveal, that there was discussion of the Report, either in the Senate proper or in its committees. It may be that there is widespread tacit acceptance of the recommendations, with general feeling that we simply act upon them as fully and quickly as we can. If so, I would like some official Senate word to that effect.

For two reasons, however, I think that blanket endorsement will not be the best way to go. First, the Report *does* indicate ranking of priorities, and I would guess that the faculty as a whole might not be in agreement with the committee on all points. Secondly, during this year we must present a ten-year plan to the Commission for Higher Education, and while its proposals will, of course, not be inflexibly binding, we should have as firm and specific a document as we can manage. Last spring we submitted a preliminary plan, but in many places it was quite general and trial-run, in part because the University as a system was seeking a workable and uniform format.

I will shortly be discussing with Dean Peyser and Professor Wolfe ways in which we might give the Priorities Report the attention it must have.

In addition to the Priorities Report, during the year just ended most of the faculty who worked on that document served again on a committee proposed by Chancellor Bowman to study Career Education—the question, basically, of how to secure a better fit between college training and available vocations. That document will shortly have appropriate distribution, and should be considered with the earlier report as work on the ten-year plan progresses.

I venture that the "half-knowledge" we have as we read what to each of us may be the best parts of the Commission's own early plan for post-secondary public education, and our impulse to counteract the disturbing parts by reaching out for "fact" and "reason" springs from our desire to nail down *exactly* what the college should be doing. When our notion of "exactly" conflicts with someone else's—particularly some one who has more power or authority—it is difficult to keep the faith and to see clearly.

My third, and concluding, matter for comment is, as I have suggested, a special instance of the curricular justifications we will be asked to make with increasing urgency in the future. As I speak, I do not know what the outcome will be of a meeting with the Program Committee of the Higher Education Commission attended a few weeks ago by Dean Peyser, Professor Demaree, and myself, along with officers from IU at Fort Wayne, and the all-University Office of Academic Affairs. We were there to defend the University's request to have degree-granting authority in music at South Bend and Fort Wayne, programs which have been carefully nurtured these past eight years, and already with several graduates who have been granted waivers of residence by the School of Music at Bloomington. Doubts have risen in the minds of some of the commissioners as to whether such degrees are appropriate at our campuses, or whether there is need for them, given the alleged availability of adequate programs at other public and private institutions around the state. The fortunes of music are our immediate concern, but no one can escape what the likely implications of a negative decision would be for the other arts in metropolitan areas around the state.

There is no reason to believe that the commissioners are anything other than able persons giving freely of their time to make the sober appraisals required of them. They have already voiced their support for continuing development of the non-residential campuses around the state. They wrestle, even as we do and must, with the problem of how best to spend the tax dollar by avoiding duplication, and by not supporting programs which lack demonstrable utility—even with the most generous definition of "utility."

The commissioners are concerned with a state-wide plan, and state-wide costs. They asked us what priority we would give music; would we, for example, support it rather than technical studies if money were available for one program, and not the other. Our position was not to allow as foregone conclusion that our state could not find means to support whatever properly belonged in the province of post-secondary education. Esoteric and highly-specialized sub-divisions of advanced study clearly cannot be offered everywhere, but surely, along with the word and the mathematical formula, musical notation and artistic line constitute the major symbols that establish our humanity. Apropos of all this, Bertrand Russell once observed that no dog, no matter how eloquently he may bark, can tell you that his parents were honest but poor.

At least one commissioner was concerned with what the citizens of Rising Sun, a small community in southeastern Indiana, would gain from the spending of dollars to support music in South Bend and Fort Wayne. We suggested that one of the reasons for developing programs where there were concentrations of population was that the talent thereby gathered could, in fact, reach out to smaller communities in many ways. And although this was aside from the tax priorities thrust of the commissioner's question, we suggested that if music should somehow be present everywhere, it would be of no aid to Rising Sun if the sun of public support for the arts should set in South Bend.

We left with the committee not only our internally generated justification and defense, but several letters from South Bend area citizens to be weighed by the Commission in the light of its own declaration that the regional campuses should contribute to the cultural life of the communities they serve. Some typical statements from those letters: "It is really impossible to tell you what a huge effect IUSB has had on the musical life of South Bend in the few short years since its beginning"; "I have been very impressed with the exceptional quality of the music department at IUSB, and also with the extent to which it is involved with the community as a whole"; "The production of *Hansel and Gretel* will have been seen by 20,000 children of South Bend schools by spring of 1973. These productions are made possible because of IUSB music majors"; ". . . music at IUSB without career possibilities would not be a serious undertaking and would never be able to do for South Bend what it is doing now." And so on, with many more letters and comments in this vein.

Uncertainties, mysteries, and doubts about the total public acceptance of our professional interests will be with us for a long time, perhaps forever. Nonetheless, in many ways we have had ample recognition for our efforts both materially and in many spontaneous expressions of appreciation for what IUSB is contributing to the lives of our students and citizens—even as they have contributed to our lives. If we minimize those genuine goods—or even deny them by feeling that any fine verisimilitude caught from the Penetralium of mystery has no enduring value until everything be rightly established, we can only be the poorer for it.

Warmest good wishes to you all at the beginning of this year we now share.

Remarks
Eighth Annual
Commencement Exercises

Athletic and Convocation Center,
May 15, 1974

Our eager pursuit of Emersonian individualism must not make us "insensitive to the mighty interdependencies that link us to heaven, earth, society, and to each other. . . ."

President Ryan, colleagues, ladies, gentlemen, and—most importantly—students of the 1974 class for whom I primarily offer these brief remarks:

For the eighth time in IUSB history a group of people bound together in a high hour of personal and institutional focus are here gathered in happy conclave. Probably no other human ceremony allows so many persons to be both the bestowers and receivers of warm recognition for the completion of sustained and critically important effort. Thus, a university commencement exercise provides a moment for each graduate that is at once intensely private and joyously communal. The communal aspect, symbolized by the robes of ancient academic tradition, the audience of family and friends, and the unifying presence of the President of our distinguished multi-campus University, combines with the individual pride each of you deserves to feel for having attained that particular corner of understanding which your degree represents.

The commingled mood of idiosyncratic worth and public harmony we feel on an occasion like this is, in a sense, the end of all learning and the necessary base for civil society. When that delicate accord breaks down, or when the personal and communal become antagonistic, we must consider—as we are considering on a dramatic scale in our country today—the extent of disruption that can be caused by serious discrepancy between magnanimous outward proclamation and inner self-serving. Men should be what they seem, Othello said, and Emerson, distinguishing between greatness and meanness observed that

> it is easy in the world to live after the world's opinion; it is easy
> in solitude to live after our own; but the great man is he who
> in the midst of the crowd keeps with perfect sweetness the
> independence of solitude.

While Emerson to some degree was decrying the crowd, and extolling the individual, we all must live in the larger world, so that if necessary devotion to a particular idea of personal space becomes obsessive in a way that makes one insensitive to the mighty interdependencies that link us to heaven, earth, society, and to each other, then everything we have done in all of our institutions has failed for that man or woman.

Last year the gifted poet W. H. Auden died, leaving a body of precisely framed utterance that remarks upon the varied orchestration of the mortal scene. A brooding generosity about the need each of us has for definition—even for psychic survival—through our unique life situation, coupled with bemused awareness of how limiting such definition can be unless by some act of capacious sympathy we can see our personal position as only one possibility among myriad others, shines through his poem "Law Like Love." A few stanzas go like this:

> Law, say the gardeners, is the sun,
> Law is the one
> All gardeners obey
> Tomorrow, yesterday, today.

Law is the wisdom of the old
The impotent grandfathers shrilly scold;
The grandchildren put out a treble tongue,
Law is the senses of the young.

Law, says the priest with a priestly look,
Expounding to an unpriestly people,
Law is the words in my priestly book,
Law is my pulpit and my steeple.

Yet law-abiding scholars write;
Law is neither wrong nor right,
Law is only crimes
Punished by places and by times,
Law is the clothes men wear
Anytime, anywhere,
Law is Good-morning and Good-night.

And always the loud angry crowd
Very angry and very loud
Law is We,
And always the soft idiot softly Me.

If IUSB has served you well, you will have the strength of your own convictions, and yet you will have openness toward others. You will have a sense of the richness and diversity present on this fragile globe we inhabit together. You will recognize in the human witness of men like Jesse Dickinson and Albert Beutler, who leaves IUSB in July to become president of Bethel College, the beautiful integration of personality that allows no distinction between what a man says, and what he is and does. Let these two represent for us how continuing intertwined personal and communal spirit can go forth from this night to suffuse all our future acts and days.

Mr. President, I now take great pleasure in presenting to you the Class of 1974 for the conferring of degrees.

Lester Wolfson with IU President John W. Ryan,
Commencement, May 13, 1987

That Our Light Be Not Darkness
Delivered at the Fall Faculty Meeting,
August 28, 1974

Ten years after Wolfson's appointment, IUSB celebrates with the other regional campuses a new "essential self-determination." Concurrently, the campus nears completion of negotiations to acquire the Associates facilities to greatly expand the scope of the campus, and its faculty undertakes the revision of its constitution. Transcending even these important steps, IUSB must still pursue its abiding goals of "freedom, equitableness, calmness, moderation, and wisdom."

Three years ago, to our graduating class of 1971 I found occasion to mention Stephen Dedalus, hero of James Joyce's *A Portrait of the Artist as a Young Man*. Stephen once wrote in a column in the flyleaf of his geography book, first his name, then in ever-widening concentric contexts, his place in a kind of spatial and psychic eternity:

Stephen Dedalus
Class of Elements
Clongowes Wood College
Sallins
County Kildare
Ireland
Europe
The World
The Universe

Over the past ten years at IUSB, I suspect that we have often
felt like a clutch of Stephen Dedali pondering the direction of our
coming-of-age within the Indiana University system. On that score,
Vice-Chancellor Rufus Reiberg of the now-defunct Regional Campus Administration used to say that the regional campuses would
ineluctably evolve into those kinds of entities they were inevitably
destined to become. Rufus's fun with the difficulties—and preten-
sions—of planning gave properly reverent respect to the "... divinity
that shapes our ends,/Roughhew them how we will." Be all this
as it may, IUSB's position has shifted dramatically in the past few
months, as for the first time in our experience we become a mature
partner in a confederation of sister campuses, with new opportunity
and responsibility devolving fully upon us. This is a grand culmina-
tion toward which—even if it has not always seemed so—President
Ryan and later Chancellor Bowman have worked unremittingly
since 1968.

The full bearings of the re-organization of the University approved
by the Trustees on June 29, 1974 will not be known for some time,
but along with the now-gained essential self-determination we have
sought for the regional campuses, in the offing there is the prospect
of a uniquely brilliant blend of program effort in a Bloomington-
Indianapolis core—effort which will be available where possible,
necessary, and desired to the rest of the system. Re-organization has
removed three parallel layers of University administration—the RCA
chancellorship, and the separate chancellorships of Bloomington and
Indianapolis. The president and vice-presidents, along with pertinent
deans, will give most of their administrative attention to the core
complex, while at the other campuses, with greatly increased authority, chancellors, deans, division heads, and faculties will be directly
charged to bring Indiana University quality to the metropolitan
areas we serve. Systemic unity and compatibility will be continued
and furthered in many ways—important among them the actions
of the all-University Faculty Council, the new formal presence of
each chancellor at Trustees meetings, and the chancellors' membership on the University Administrative, Board Agenda, Long-Range
Planning, and Budget Committees. Through such immediate repre-
sentation, the position of our campus can be directly conveyed, and

we will have far more informed understanding of concerns, prospects, and limitations that affect all campuses of the University.

This major change in our operational status coincidentally—maybe providentially—has arrived when the long-sought solution to our need for added functional and aesthetic space is highly probable, indeed imminent. Negotiations between the University and the Associates are reaching final stages. If a transaction can be consummated, IUSB will gain excellently built and engineered facilities at a fraction of the

Administration Building, acquired from the Associates Corp.
Wiekamp Hall has not yet been built.

cost to citizens and students of comparable new construction. Moreover, after years of uncertainty, the total outline of our campus site will assume final form as we look to the remainder of this century. If we acquire these extensive properties, proposed assignment and adaptation of space will need our collective serious attention in the months and years before occupancy is secured. Compromises may have to be worked out as to the ideal shape of things, but I hope the consensus will be that this route promises far more for the strength of IUSB than any feasible alternative. If Wallace Stevens could find thirteen ways of looking at a blackbird, we might find one true notion of truth in the jingle:

Truth ever lies in mean compromise
Said Sam Butler:

What could be subtler
Than the thought of Sam Butler?

Apart from the major questions of University re-organization and the Associates, I should like to mention briefly several other items of general concern. Elaboration on some of these topics will occur in upcoming Senate meetings, in the Newsletter, and in the Quarterly Status Quote, which will be revived next month.

Most important, I think, is the proposed revision of the IUSB Faculty Constitution, which has served us well in its nearly ten years of present form, but clearly needs modifications. The draft I have seen incorporates policies and procedures that have been tested by experience as we have felt and thought our way toward this ripe hour. Second, the five member colleges of NICE—the Northern Indiana Consortium for Education—have very recently appointed an Executive Director through a grant from the Lilly Endowment. Local institutional program, student, and faculty cooperation should be greatly enhanced by the presence of a full-time executive. St. Mary's College is serving as fiscal agent, while IUSB will provide space for the director and his staff. Third, with George Wing's assistance, I plan soon to appoint a committee to be concerned with priorities and long-range planning, as mentioned in my response of last January to the earlier report prepared by the labors of our then ad hoc Committee on Priorities. Administratively, as required by the Higher Education Commission we have recently submitted a ten-year plan to the Office of the President—a plan which at the moment is largely a statistical exercise built upon a University-wide premise of little over-all enrollment change during the next decade. I do not think that the premise is correct for IUSB, but whether it is or isn't, obviously the hard work of attending to program growth, preservation, and maybe pruning remains before us. Let me interject here a word about program: we currently have several degree proposals pending before the Higher Education Commission. All are important, but if you will recall the remarks I made about music a year ago, and my statement about fine arts last January, you will know why I think it is particularly critical that the BA in Fine Arts be approved at the earliest possible time.

With some trepidation I mention parking and hot-food service, since somehow I manage never to say the right thing on those heads. I'm not sure whether it represents progress to say we now have a paid parking plan, but we *do* have one, with rates set as low as possible to make needed improvements and to allow for proper amortization. As to hot food, I had better not lead a guided tour to the old vending area in the student lounge: I simply ask that you look at the pipe and drain work in order to draw your own conclusions. (By the way, if we do acquire the Associates property, cafeteria and other food service capabilities will compare favorably with those to be found almost anywhere.)

Whatever the seeming hydra-headed problems and—more often—mere annoyances which exist in any given year, or from year to year, I think that the IUSB community has shown itself able to approach them all in a spirit of remarkable accord. But since there are sometimes real toads in real gardens, when accord breaks down it is not always because—in the cliché of our time—we have not "communicated" enough. Nonetheless, I imagine no one will pretend that we have found the best forums for sharing our common concern about the welfare of IUSB. I believe we have made some right moves in sharing budgetary matters with the faculty. Students, I think, have equal right to know about the allocation of resources, and I will ask Mike Phebus and his associates to let me know how we can be helpful there. Through the Committee on Teaching and the Course Evaluation Handbook we have made some progress in the assessment of teaching, but sometimes students, faculty, and administrators have worked at cross purposes, or at least in too great isolation. I hope that this year there can be a united approach in devising procedures that will so far as possible be acceptable to all parties in making the judgments that should be made. Whether this can be best done through the Student Affairs Committee, or at specified times in the actual deliberations of the Academic Senate, I urge the faculty to help me in disabusing students of any lingering notion that the administration "tells" the faculty what to do—any more than the most reflective students would want any of us to "tell" them what to do.

I hope that what has been said to this point makes some sense, but I would feel best if you are sharing my impatience that much of what has been talked about so far is machinery or represents a kind of ritualistic tap-dancing. Any of us, not only the young, can be tempted to neglect monuments of unaging intellect. What difference do all the permutations of faculty organization, administrative structure, number and size of committees, and every variant of institutional rigmarole make when we recall the salutary uses of mind to which every good college is dedicated?

Reading many of the volumes that treat of higher education today can be a vastly depressing experience. The intent is earnest, the social concern genuine, the balancing of finances necessary, but there is so little joy or even enthusiasm expressed for that power of the mind which derives satisfaction from seeing things steadily and seeing them whole. We have worked hard at IUSB to extend the number of studies offered here, sometimes to be sure out of parochial intent, but more often, I venture, since many of us have felt with Cardinal Newman that enlarging the range of studies which a university professes is good for the students because even ". . . though they cannot pursue every subject which is open to them, they will be gainers by living among those and under those who represent the whole circle." John Henry Newman saw a true faculty as an "assemblage of learned men, zealous for their own sciences, and rivals of each other . . ." who "are brought, by familiar intercourse and for the sake of intellectual peace, to adjust together the claims and relations of their respective subjects of investigation. They learn to respect, to consult, to aid each other."

Even if this ideal has been only partially realized in any given institution, the student gains because there will be "a pure and clean atmosphere of thought, which the student also breathes, though in his own case he only pursues a few sciences out of the multitude." As for the various cults of personality, a school which respects the claims of its disciplines will profit the student

> by an intellectual tradition, which is independent of particular teachers, which guides him in his choice of subjects, and duly interprets for him those which he chooses. He apprehends the great outlines of knowledge, the principles on which it rests, the scale of its parts, its lights and its shades, its great points and its little, as he otherwise cannot apprehend them. Hence

it is that his education is called "liberal." A habit of mind is formed which lasts through life, of which the attributes are freedom, equitableness, calmness, moderation, and wisdom. . . . Knowledge is capable of being its own end. Such is the constitution of the human mind that any kind of knowledge, if it be really such, is its own reward.

Newman is in the great tradition, too rarely appealed to these days, which believes in the formative effect on character—though not finally on the soul—of liberal education, the purpose of which is to make the gentleman (the gentle man) who will have "a cultivated intellect, a delicate taste, a candid, equitable, dispassionate mind, a noble and courteous bearing in the conduct of life . . . the connatural qualities of a large knowledge." While such qualities tend to make the good man, as well as the gentleman, intellectual excellence alone can make no guarantee of goodness, for only if you can

Quarry the granite rock with razors, or moor the vessel with a thread of silk . . . may you hope with such keen and delicate instruments as human knowledge and human reason to contend against those giants, the passion and the pride of man.

But for Newman, intellect has its special beauty:

To open the mind, to correct it, to refine it, to enable it to know, and to digest, master, rule, and use its knowledge, to give it power over its own faculties, application, flexibility, method, critical exactness, sagacity, resource, address, eloquent expression, is . . . an object as intelligible as the cultivation of virtue, while, at the same time, it is absolutely distinct from it.

Newman's language may strike some as a bit archaic, but how splendidly he helps us to recall the delights of liberal study. To read or hear Shakespeare is to have an experience with language that resounds in the very way one breathes. To begin to understand even vaguely the binary system of mathematics that makes computer science possible and intelligible; to see the structure of matter pictured in the mobiles that might double as futuristic art; to know something of DNA and what it portends for our understanding of genetic mysteries; to feel the clean inevitability of a syllogism in logic; to appreciate the rhetorical elegance of "We hold these truths to be self-evident"; to understand the religious fervor and literary grace of "Thou hast made us for Thyself, O Lord, and our heart is restless until it finds rest again in Thee"—to know all these things is to be enlarged and enriched beyond speakable measure. The prime reason for our institutional existence is to serve these good ends for our students and ourselves. After basic material needs have been provided for, surely all significant utility flows from such informed awareness.

In the classic Chapter IV, "Hebraism and Hellenism," from *Culture and Anarchy*, Matthew Arnold cites Bishop Thomas Wilson, an early eighteenth century divine: "First, never go against the best light you have; secondly, take care that your light be not darkness." Applying this thought to Victorian England Arnold said, "We show, as a nation, laudable energy and persistence in walking according to the best light we have, but are not quite careful enough, perhaps, to see that our light be not darkness." To illumine the intellect of students is the fundamental charge of educators. None of us can do so if we insist too strenuously on the vanity of formal pecking-orders or non-human territorial imperatives where raw energy is mistaken for true light.

Ten years ago as Director and Assistant Dean, in the first talk I was privileged to give to the faculty of what was then the South Bend-Mishawaka Campus of Indiana University, I ventured to say that although we are a secular institution, we have a sacred charge, that whatever our particular discipline, our passion for intellectual order is akin to all other concerns for the spirit. Ten years of experience with good colleagues and generations of students have strengthened my feeling that despite occasional jockeying and pointless contention this search for order remains our distinguishing mark. The Elizabethans believed that "Order of all beauties the greatest beauty is." In whatever measure we can rise to an integrated view of knowledge, we will have had the best sublunary equivalent of the vision Dante had at the conclusion of the *Paradiso*, when in the depths of the eternal light he saw "ingathered, bound by love in one volume, the scattered leaves of all the universe; substance and accidents and their relations, as though together fused, after such fashion that what I tell of is one simple flame."

Let our most promising year at IUSB now begin.

Kind Hearts Are More than Coronets
Delivered at the Fall Faculty Meeting,
September 3, 1975

In addition to the newly-created resident string quartet and the Honors Program, the campus pursues its identity as a metropolitan university. It must become a community of ages, employment, and family interaction that grows through all the stages of life. IUSB's curriculum and program scheduling must be both more flexible and more systematic.

Some months ago one of our arts and sciences chairmen told me he had discovered what it meant to be crushed between upper and nether millstones. Mary Ellen Hegedus has been gentle enough in her remarks just concluded, but I fear I might be zapped by George Wing since he has filched the title of his forthcoming address from me, after I had stolen my title from one of Tennyson's lesser verses, "Lady Clara Vere de Vere." That jingle contains the lines which served as epigraph to the classic motion picture comedy *Kind Hearts and Coronets*, in which a poor youth—like the speaker in the poem—loves and aspires above his station:

Trust me, Clara Vere de Vere,
    From yon blue heavens above us bent
The gardener Adam and his wife
    Smile at the claims of long descent.
Howe'er it be, it seems to me,
    'Tis only noble to be good.
Kind hearts are more than coronets,
    And simple faith than Norman blood.

I don't know what George is going to do with "'Tis only noble to be good," but I will attempt in the last section of these remarks to derive some pertinence out of hearts and coronets. Let me now, however, give a summary reprise of the year just ended, with first the good news, and—then—some more good news.

A major happening, which will have great impact on academic development and physical amenities at IUSB, was the purchase of the land and buildings comprising the home headquarters of the Associates Corporation of North America. The advantages to IUSB of that transaction have already been comprehensively chronicled in extensive spreads in the *South Bend Tribune*, primarily on December 12, 1974 and February 9, 1975. There is no need here to rehearse all the particulars, but we now have the missing dimensions in the critical mass required to provide for practically all of our foreseeable programs for the rest of the century. What remains to be done in the near future before we secure our first occupancy in less than three years is to re-design our total plat, and to plan for the most effective placement of institutional functions in the new property.

A second major happening, although with less immediately visible effect, was the unfolding throughout the year of what now can be seen as the clear implications of the dissolution of Regional Campus Administration as an intermediate layer between our campus and system-wide offices in the distinguished University of which we are an increasingly integral and valuable part. If the remaining judgmental, managerial, and review functions which RCA had maintained in some degree to the very end of its existence had simply been shifted to the President's office, the ripe hour of maturity we have reached would have been hampered in its scope and significance. That shifting has not occurred, and we are now ready to enjoy and to cultivate the fruits which have had their seeds in the decades-long history of Indiana University. Poet Delmore Schwartz once wrote that in dreams begin responsibilities. Our dream for IUSB as an ever-stronger center of teaching and learning has now placed upon us the responsibility of intensified commitment to the need to know securely, to feel precisely, and to act joyously.

In recognition of the truth in the aphorism that only as we are bound are we truly free, we should be able to accept the systemic policies of a major University—now well into the second century of its history—as support and warrant of the freedom we have to determine our own campus priorities in a way that will serve the dual needs of intellectual tradition and contemporary pragmatic relevance. At IUSB, the on-going tasks of establishing or reaffirming those priorities, and of bringing them to the light of day, will be a co-operative endeavor of teaching faculty, administrative faculty, other officers, and students alike. This will be expressed not only formally in the work of the Academic Senate, the Committee on Long-Range Planning, the Student Association, and the Inter-University deliberations of system-wide bodies and councils, but also in open-door practices of informal access so that intuitive inspiration not be vagrant.

The new confidence we all feel in our talent and strength has been, and increasingly will be, vindicated by elements we are adding to our program that lessen whatever threat of provincialism hovers near our regional setting. For example, Professors Beardsley, Scherer, Schreiber, Tawadros, and Thorson—to name only a few—have studied, taught, or participated in international symposia in Europe this past year. A distinguished African sculptor, Francis Nnaggenda, was a visiting professor at IUSB during the spring term. To encourage the growth of such activity, we hope soon to establish a separate budget for International Programs. The initial sums available will be modest, but I dare say that there will be inexorable impetus for steady growth. A related development is our recent appointment of a remarkably proficient young string ensemble, the International Quartet, whose members have antecedents of family and training in Germany, Japan, and the United States. In yet another kind of reach, we have established an Honors Division program and budget, under the directorship of Professor Furlong, which will provide special opportunities for our most able students and complement existing programs that give help to the student who is less well prepared. I anticipate that programs for the intellectually gifted, like our international programs, will flourish, adding to the contributions which so many of you have made in various readings courses and in individual attention you have given to academically superior students. IUSB, in all the ways proper to it, must be a house with many rooms.

I tried to catch the spirit of this indispensable multi-faceted cooperative endeavor in my remarks to our first graduating class on June 7, 1967, by saying that "No one knows better than University people that history is not the lengthened shadow of one man but is, rather, if a happy history, the happy confluence of many contributing streams of mind and heart." This past year, the closing of ranks so willingly in the face of unusual trials which beset some of our key people, demonstrated as graphically as anything I can recall in my eleven years here such truth as those remarks might have. I know that you rejoice with me at the restoration to us, after serious illness, of John Cassidy, valued senior member of this faculty. I record here my deep gratitude to Joe Peyser for the perceptive contributions he made to the Dean of Faculties' office in preparation for our new degree of autonomy before considerations of health obliged him to leave that office. I am delighted that continuity in so important an assignment will be maintained by our having found within our own numbers so able a person as Jerry Harriman, who for nine years gave strong and even-handed leadership to the Division of Business and Economics.

In singling out these few of our colleagues for specific mention, I do not imply that you or I are unaware of the contributions scores have made to the total dignity of our campus. I shall touch upon a few of those accomplishments a bit later, but an apt summing up of our present status appears in the North Central Association's listed reasons for granting this summer continued accreditation of IUSB programs at all levels through the spring of 1980: "Basic strength of institutional faculty and administrative staff, excellent physical plant potential, sound programs generally. . . ."

So much for the reprise. What tasks lie ahead?

In his book, *The Divided Self*, R. D. Laing tells of a schizophrenic patient whose psychiatrist attaches him to a lie detector. When the doctor asks the patient if he is really Napoleon, the patient says "no," whereupon the polygraph instantly registers that he is lying. I am not quite sure what that all means. It might mean that we shouldn't trust machines, or it might demonstrate again the elementary proposition that the strength of a conviction is no warranty of its truth. In any event, the shaggy dog aspects of the story make me a little reticent about attempting grand proclamations, which may turn out to be only grandiose. Nonetheless, I predict that our efforts to gain more recognition and support for IUSB—both from the legislature and from private sources—will meet with accelerating success in the financial activity of each succeeding year.

I say this not only because the demand for our programs has reached an all-time peak this present semester, but also because there are many subtle and overt signs that the desirable linkage of universities and metropolitan areas is making steady advance against the old notion that the real—or at least the most valuable—college experience can be obtained only at a residential campus. Life may well be a series of stages, but it need and ought not to be a series of compartments where four years, typically between 18-22, are blocked out for some kind of experience called "going to college." Nor should older people feel that "everything else" must be gotten out of the way before they can seek the nurturing which only formal learning experience imparts. Increasingly, progress on the human fronts of work, study, and family interaction will be made simultaneously rather than sequentially. To make our contribution to this new style of living we must be more flexible and more systematic. One form of flexibility will come in even better management of space, time, and instructional modes than has marked us to this point; one form of greater system will be in the designing of courses of study that will enable the part-time student to know that over a period of years he can complete specific programs. Jim Ryan, along with several others of you, has worked diligently on these questions this past year, and we hope to have many specific applications available by the 1976-77 school year.

The adapting of our operations to these varying life patterns must be done without any sacrifice of respect for the inherent controlling demands of the intellectual, aesthetic, and professional disciplines. Nor can these adaptations come at the cost of—indeed, they can only spring from—profound respect for the intrinsic worth and possibility of each of our students and each of our colleagues. We have made some advance, not yet sufficient, on alleviating the problems of those who have been restricted to ghettos of the spirit, which demean persons because of extraneous definitions by sex, race, religion, and age. We must heed not only what our own best contemporaries are telling us about full equality for women, for example, but also what New

Englander Margaret Fuller wrote in the early 19th century: "What woman needs, is not as a woman to act or rule, but as a nature to grow, as an intellect to discern, as a soul to live freely, and unimpeded to unfold such powers as were given her."

To help all of our students to unfold these powers, with whatever cognitive-affective balance may be best, is our first charge. And while we cannot be indifferent to the present crisis in careers and income—upon which careers and income so much of one's sense of self depends—we cannot let those considerations detract in any way from the conviction that our primary mission is continuously to imbue our students and ourselves with the liberating and refreshing sense of worth which springs from wide reference and informed understanding. The furniture of the mind remains more important than the furniture in a house. Even as we work to assist our students in career development and job placement, such efforts should not take priority over the faith that our fields of study are necessary ends in themselves. And even as we recognize the current economic needs of our students, or make institutional bows in the direction of whatever in the pop culture of art and thought is momentarily attractive, we might recall what literary scholar Howard Mumford Jones has said:

> Our responsibility is civil, not whimsical, our business is with time and eternity, our converse should be with kings of thought, not with entertainers a la mode.

I hope what has been said to this point will now suggest that we need no dichotomies of kind hearts or coronets—no denigration of either simple goodness or of what is genuinely aristocratic. The rightful claims of long descent—of hierarchy, structure, tradition—can exist comfortably with the more mundane aspects of democratic relationships. The full energies of a place like IUSB can be directed at the same time toward serious disciplinary study and toward quickening the material well-being and total competence of the community in which we live. During the past year, for example, Warren Pepperdine was instrumental in helping to reject an alien New York vision of stage design which would have seriously reduced the versatility for local use of the theatre which will be constructed in Century Center.

And while the issue is not yet fully resolved, at the moment it appears as if our economists Paul Joray and Paul Kochanowski have played a determining role in working together with labor and the Chamber of Commerce in preventing the abandonment of many miles of railroad lines, which might have had a more disastrous economic impact on our region than the closing of Studebaker over a decade ago. In fact, a high officer of the University of Notre Dame has recently indicated that Notre Dame will be saved about $500,000 a year by not having to resort to other means of coal delivery. I don't imagine that Notre Dame would give any of those savings to an IUSB development fund, but I do know that through the contribution the faculty of IUSB so abundantly makes our stature grows, and our proper pride develops.

This is an inspiriting time to be at Indiana University at South Bend. There is no question but that we have become a major force, not only in the greater capability with which we teach our immediate students, but also as a prime contributor to elevating the quality of life for miles around. Obviously, we have many laurels yet to win, and it will be a long time before we can consider resting on those laurels.

In Shakespeare's *Troilus and Cressida*, Achilles bemoans his passing fame, asking, "What, are my deeds forgot?" To which the wise Ulysses responds:

> Time hath, my lord, a wallet at his back
> Wherein he puts alms for oblivion,
> A great-sized monster of ingratitudes.
> Those scraps are good deeds past, which are devoured
> As fast as they are made, forgot as soon
> As done. Perseverance, dear my lord,
> Keeps honor bright. To have done is to hang
> Quite out of fashion, like a rusty mail
> In monumental mockery.

IUSB has persevered in all manner of honorable tasks of teaching, learning, and serving. We will never be done and hang out of fashion. We are getting close to 1990, which by most general reckoning will be the 50th anniversary of our organized existence. When that history is written, it will be replete with high moments of personal and collective accomplishment. I comfortably believe that 1975-76 will be one of the brightest years to be recorded in that history, and I am glad to begin it with you now.

Reflections upon Returning
Delivered at an IUSB Faculty Meeting,
February 8, 1980

Reflections on a six-month sabbatical in England, France, and Italy, and the consequent sense of history "both cruel and kind," inform a recognition of IUSB's past achievements and confidence in its continuing promise.

When John Lewis asked if I wished any special format for this part of today's meeting I perhaps too quickly suggested that he schedule these remarks as "Reflections Upon Returning." Since then I've had a little trouble with the specific meaning I intended for "returning." I have returned to office; I have returned from Europe; I have returned (in part) from a six-month psychological distancing that has lent renewed enchantment to my view of life's possibilities. Moreover, I think that maybe I am now grown old enough to understand what Tennyson's Ulysses meant when he said,

I am a part of all that I have met,
Yet all experience is an arch wherethrough
Gleams that untraveled world whose margin fades
Forever and forever when I move.

As with the lover in John Donne's famous poem, for me absence from accustomed haunts and duties and affections was not a breach, but an expansion. And I understand more than ever what William Hazlitt felt in saying "I should . . . like well enough to spend the whole of my life in traveling abroad, if I could anywhere borrow another life to spend afterwards at home."

I feel my psyche in some small but significant way was changed in Rome on Friday, September 21, 1979, the day of the eve of Rosh Hashonah—the Jewish New Year—when, as I rode in bus 64 on the way to St. Peter's and the Vatican Museums, my traveler's checks were stolen. Comforted by the thought of Karl Malden, later that same day I met a smiling official in the American Express office at the Spanish Steps who with little delay replaced them all. I then walked some five or six doors away where the Keats-Shelley Memorial occupies the house Keats arrived at over 150 years ago in vain search for something far more precious than lost checks. The Pieta, the Basilica, the Sistine Chapel, the sense of a holy day coming, being robbed, looking out the window through which Keats last looked—what a compression of world, fate, and time into something akin for me to Blake's having seen eternity in a grain of sand!

The day before, on a beautiful morning, I was the only one present at the Protestant Cemetery. There, in viewing Keats's grave, with its moving inscription ending "Here lies One/Whose name was writ in Water," I thought of the time more than twenty years earlier when at the Lilly Library in Bloomington I had read one of Keats's letters to Fanny Brawne in which he said to her, with poignant understatement, that he was not getting any better. And Shelley's tomb a few score yards away, with its lines cited from Shakespeare, "Nothing of him that doth fade,/But doth suffer a sea-change/Into something rich and strange," recalled *his* letter, also in the Lilly Library, wherein—ironically as it turned out—Shelley praised the shipbuilder for the seaworthiness of the ship in which he shortly thereafter drowned.

There were lighter considerations too. The staggering ruins of the Coliseum prompted me to write Jerry Harriman and the gang on the second floor-front asking if we *really* wanted a "multi-purpose recreational facility." And from Blarney Castle in Ireland I wrote one card home saying that I had seen, but not kissed, the legended stone for fear of 1) contracting a meretricious disease, and 2) falling.

I carried no camera, but I did keep a diary reflecting on the Santa Croce Church in Florence, where Michelangelo, Galileo, Machiavelli, and Rossini are buried; the Borghese gardens and gallery in Rome; the Louvre; Versailles; the Rodin Museum; the Paris Opera with its incongruent but gorgeous Chagall ceiling, where Joe Peyser and I saw a splendid *Faust*; the special greenness of Ireland, made magical by soft suffusing rain; Dublin's fair city; the Scottish Highlands; Notre Dame, Coventry, Exeter, and Winchester Cathedrals, as well as dozens more overwhelming in their concept and execution; the Lake Country so rightly loved and celebrated by Wordsworth and Coleridge; Edinburgh, Plymouth, Bath, Stratford, and Windsor; the inexhaustible treasures of London. And everywhere the all-pervasive sense of history, both cruel and kind.

I know that your similar experiences have confirmed in you, as they did in me, an awareness of how critical our enterprise as educators is, as we study the tradition of art, intellect, and social order; contribute to it; and convey it to our students and society at large. At first try, in routine or the fog and traffic of struggle and contention that smother the spirit, it may be hard to relate what in some measure are holiday impressions to on-going daily effort. That, too, requires some perspective afforded by standing back and summing up.

At IUSB we have such an opportunity this very year occasioned by the forthcoming reaccreditation visit in April by the North Central Association. The self-study required by that visit, building on the results of the "IUSB: Toward the Future" discussions of last year, presents a convincing picture of a campus doing many things remarkably well, and fully aware of ways and means to do them better. Many of you have contributed to that effort, skillfully co-ordinated and written by Karen Rasmussen, and recently sent off to the appropriate places. In time all of you here will have a personal copy or ready access to the complete report. The narrative now completed is lucid and comprehensive, documenting accomplishment and purpose in which we can all take pride. A few selected representative excerpts will demonstrate:

> Since 1975 faculty from the Division of Business and Economics have published four books, reviewed manuscripts for five national journals and guest-edited one of them, held fellowships from the Lilly Endowment and the Brookings Institute and consultancies or other positions with the National Aeronautical and Space Administration, the Department of Housing and Urban Development, and the State Department's AID Program.

The Division of Music has hired faculty who bring national reputations with them and who continue to perform to that same high standard after joining IUSB. Six of these faculty have toured extensively, both in the states and abroad. Our pianist-in-residence has performed and recorded in London, for example, and in 1978 our former member of the Hamburg Opera sang a series of recitals in Italy. Also in 1978, the International String Quartet played forty concerts outside of South Bend and contracted to record the complete Mozart String Quartets for Vox Productions.

Arts and Sciences faculty are correspondingly productive within the scholarly requirements of fourteen different disciplines. Members of the Chemistry Department have presented eighteen papers over the past five years, two of them at overseas conferences. Mathematics faculty have published 14 papers since 1977-78, and Philosophy faculty, 13. Since 1977 two historians have published books. One member of the English Department obtained a 1978-79 Lilly Endowment fellowship to study filmmaking. National Science Foundation grants went to a mathematician and a philosopher. Members of the History and Communication Arts departments received NEH fellowships for 1979. One historian received the Leverhulme Prize for 1978-79, another received the Rome Prize, and two colleagues became co-editors of the Biography Series sponsored by the Conference on British Studies. In collaboration with Continuing Education an Earth Sciences faculty member obtained federal funding for "Project Effect," an energy conservation education program; as a result of the reputation which IUSB acquired through that project's activities, the campus has received additional funding to establish a regional Center for Energy Conservation.

To the fine record of scholarship and disciplinary performance that distinguishes the IUSB faculty can be added the pleasingly significant fact that in the past eight years, six of our colleagues have won all-University distinguished teaching awards—a number greater than that from the five other Indiana University regional campuses combined.

Our accomplishment deserves, and gets, unrelenting if not always successful advocacy from the officers charged with securing the support that a continuing first-rate effort needs, as well as the added support necessary to bring things not yet first-rate to that status. We should know very soon the level of improvement to be expected for 1980-81 over already existing appropriations and other sources of income. And the 1981-83 biennial request and justification to be completed later this year will define once again as vigorously as our collective brains will allow what the tremendous benefits of higher education are, and what commitment, both in finances and understanding, should be made to it.

As to the unfinished business at IUSB of private fund-raising—first, I have recently spoken with President Ryan about our desire to develop staff as soon as possible in the most appropriate way to lend assistance to such an effort once we have met our responsibility to state both the short- and long-range goals of this new thrust. He is sympathetic. Such delay as there might be will be occasioned only by the need to wait resolution of thinking going on even now about the dimensions of a major campaign that will involve the entire University. Secondly, I have invited Mr. William Armstrong, President of the Indiana University Foundation, to come to South Bend in the latter part of March to meet with the fifteen-person Foundation Board whose membership we plan to announce coincident with Mr. Armstrong's visit.

Another concern that has caused understandable anxiety and impatience, particularly in the last year and a half, should soon be disposed of. My understanding is that in early September the Associates engaged Arthur Andersen and Company to study the question of how the computer operation presently housed in our red brick building could best be continued and located. My further understanding is that the results of the study will be presented in Dallas next week. Our position, of course, remains exactly what it has always been. We needed a library; we still need one—worse than ever; and we expect to have one, either in the accounting building or in a new structure—properly placed—that will be as good as, or better than, what we can already count on through the decision to buy that we made five years ago.

There is another element in our position, also consistently held and announced: as citizens of our region, we want to do everything we prudently can to make it possible for the Associates to stay in our community. But we will not deviate in any way from our intent to have as scheduled the higher educational facilities vital for the well-being of north central Indiana not only now but for untold generations to come.

Thinking that there may be several things of interest to you that I have not touched upon, I have intentionally left these prepared remarks briefer than those I have given every fall from 1964 to 1978 when, the time and the purpose of the meetings being somewhat different, questions were not part of the proceedings. Before I invite such questions as then might be, let me here make public record of my deep gratitude to Dean Harriman and to Dean Rasmussen for their conduct of two offices, rather than one, in a way that made it possible for me so comfortably to take so extended a leave. I know that what they did was abetted mightily by the efforts of this faculty, in overall capability and dedication second to none in our University system. I am most happy to be back with you, and to repeat this morning what I said on September 19, 1964, early in my first talk as then-Director and Assistant Dean: "I have no adequate words to state my pleasure at the prospect of serving Indiana University with you in the future."

A Manifest Sign
Delivered at the Fall Faculty Meeting,
September 3, 1982

IUSB's history articulates the companionship of wisdom and cheerfulness, despite the current "budget vise" and an impasse in funding for a free-standing library. In the face of economic expediency, the university remains "a house of full intellect, where reason, imagination, and humane concern are honored."

It wasn't Peter Piper's, but a certain sometimes acerbic Serb's assertion that Montaigne was wrong in maintaining that "the most manifest sign of wisdom is a continual cheerfulness." The Lawrence Clipper, our ministering gadfly, thus implies that, rather than a sign of wisdom, perpetual good cheer more often signifies terminal fatuity. Larry of course speaks true, but it is a truth on the order of saying that just as profound activity marks the mind of the genius, so something or other is always going on in the head of the village idiot.

Which reality, in short, should persistently command our attention at IUSB: the growth in range and quality of program in the fifteen years since we granted our first degrees; the development of our physical plant; the recognition we have received in all-University forums for the excellence of our teaching; the recent *South Bend Tribune* editorial commendation of our latest achievements in scholarship and artistic endeavor, achievements which I have more fully chronicled in an article to appear in a special section of the October *Indiana Alumni Magazine*. Or, should our prevailing mood be determined by the flattening of enrollments; the press of the budgetary vise; the library and laboratory impasse; the seeming decline of respect for intellectual virtues and values.

In addressing these obdurate problems, there are moments when one feels like studying chicken entrails, or taking a few slugs of Mammy's Kickapoo joy juice, waiting for Yokum's moon, then doing some dervish spins in the hope of coming up with happy solutions. But the American faith in astrology notwithstanding, such routes will not avail. Let me be as forthright about these problems as I know how to be.

You may recall that in my Quarterly Report for June I said that a long-term lease with Associates appeared imminent, although funds for a new library were not at present among those being requested by the University for the 1983-85 biennium. In fact, only five of some thirty capital projects proposed University-wide were approved by the Trustees. The approval came after President Ryan said at the June Board meeting in Fort Wayne that all thirty were deserving, though prudence dictated that only a small number should be advanced. On Monday of this week, the same awareness of the state's economic condition influenced the shape of the operating request approved for 1983-85. The request reflected a second major paring down of the original budgets proposed by the various campuses of the University, but still asks for state appropriations which in 1984-85 would be some 29% higher for the system (30.46% for IUSB) than they are in 1982-83.

As to our long-standing canker, during part of a visit to South Bend yesterday, President Ryan and Executive Vice President Pinnell heard some of our academic administrators earnestly advocate yet once again the library and laboratory cause. Their response was sympathetic, if not totally empathic. In time, I suspect that a tripod of state support, application of rent, and private giving will bring us to the land of our heart's desire. But for the moment, please understand that just as within University policy I, always with your help, finally have to decide what the balances will be at our campus, so President Ryan must decide what they will be among all the campuses of the IU system. He has the additional task of persuading the Commission for Higher Education and the General Assembly of overall University needs. Probably none of us, no matter what the level of our institutional responsibility, fully escapes some uncertainty as to what the best strategy is for gaining satisfaction of our wants. But if we have due respect for the views (and the power) of others, it might be useful to recall the cartoon which shows an anxious waiter hovering over a lone diner in a posh restaurant. The caption reads: "Tell me, sir, did I walk that fine line between elegant service and fawning obsequiousness."

As to the budgetary vise, even if the outcome of our appropriation request is favorable, at IUSB we are faced with reducing our present base by some three or four percent over the next few years. The main reason is that enrollments in the recent past have not been as high as earlier projected (although this year we did hit the mark set), while budgets were developed on the assumption of higher fee income than was realized.

The matter is distressing, but not disastrous. Attrition takes care of some of the problem; we have suggestions for economies that have been made by the Planning Committee after it had gathered information from academic and administrative units; we will explore the possibility of additional income from sources other than fees; and *nothing* of any significant consequence will be decided without the full participation of the Budget Committee, and the entire Academic Senate if needed. Unfavorable appropriations will compound the difficulty, but there is no way we can expect to be exempt from the economic woes plaguing state treasuries nearly everywhere.

I will not wrong this essentially festive occasion by introducing further pestilential vapors, adding only that we think we are on firm ground University-wide in assuming level enrollments for the 1983-85 period. When the funds are available—as they surely will be in time—and we at IUSB can add the programs now missing from our curriculum, the upward trend we experienced in the '60s and '70s will return.

The financial situation in Indiana has led Governor Orr and others to suggest to the public universities, when requesting new programs or deciding upon internal reallocations, that they demonstrate what the direct bearing of such moves will be on helping the immediate economic needs of the state. This is a laudable motive, one we have not been indifferent to in the past, as we are not indifferent to it now. Our request for additional funding for the nursing program, a new electrical engineering technology program, and the already approved degree in computer science are instances of our response.

In addition, last April I convened a meeting of local government, business, labor, industrial, and collegiate educational leaders to discuss preliminarily ways in which the colleges might aid our region in spurring economic development. We expect to have a structure in place soon which will enable us to follow through in this endeavor. We have never lacked willingness at IUSB to do everything we appropriately can to improve the overall well-being of the community we live in, and upon whose backing—moral and financial—we will depend ever more heavily in the future.

There are, however, some worrisome indications that economic expediency may come to be the order of the day, that what we treasure most about the university—its being, in Len Fleck's fine phrase, a home for "the neutral conversation which makes civilization possible"—may be seen as dispensable or at best peripheral. Amidst all the necessary talk about priorities, I think we who deeply care about it will be called upon to state and restate again and again the one a priori priority: that a university is first and foremost a house of full intellect, where reason, imagination, and humane concern are honored, where the arts and sciences, from *a* to *z*, alpha to omega, in themselves and in their applications to the learned professions are preserved, refined, conveyed, and enlarged through our teaching and scholarship. No other agency or entity in our society is formed so uniquely to do this mortal work.

I fear there are currently abroad minimalist notions of "service" that may unduly influence public policy for the regional campuses. While IUSB may never be known throughout the galaxy as the Athens of the St. Joe, I see no reason why we shouldn't stay at least as good as we are—better, become better than we are. We will probably increase our efficiency—maybe, in some respects, even our effectiveness—as technology helps us convey information and technique to larger numbers of students at smaller unit cost. But I hope the day will never come when Cardinal Newman's insight is obsolete. He writes that when students seriously want to be educated, when they aim at something precise, something refined, something really luminous, something really large, something choice, they avail themselves ... of the ancient method of oral instruction, of present communication between man and man, of teachers. . . . If we wish to become exact and fully furnished in any subject of teaching which is diversified and complicated, we must consult the living man and listen to his living voice. . . . The general principles of any study you may learn by books at home; but the detail, the color, the tone, the air, the life which makes it live in us, you must catch all these from those in whom it lives already.

Newman's praise for the vivifying power of great teaching surely strikes responsive chords at this campus, where I would think our record of instructional excellence is clear and unequivocal. Yet I am told that there is some feeling that teaching is not sufficiently appreciated or rewarded at IUSB, a feeling probably intensified by what some see as my nit-picking resistance to our establishing a local distinguished teaching award. Some of my concerns are that we have done very well in a wider field of judgment; that university-level teaching is always given serious weight in matters of promotion, tenure, and retention; and that our relative smallness might better suggest a distinguished faculty award, where triple-threat colleagues would get the special recognition they would eminently merit.

All these reasons, however, may only be rationalizations springing from my ageless attachment to Alice in Wonderland's litany about unbirthdays, and from a personal experience which seemed marvelous to me at the time, but whose relevance to adult life is dubious. Many years ago, my father used to take my brother and me to the annual Elks father-and-son banquet. We had unlimited ice cream, hot dogs, and soda pop; played pool and the pinball machines; watched a smiling clown ride a unicycle; and then—best of all—gathered for the drawing which would award prizes. Just as in Norman Rockwell's world there are no stinkers, so in that drawing there were no losers. Numbers or names—I forget which—were pulled until every boy had "won" a prize. Have we come to expect so much, and so far lost our innocence that in 1982 potential legions of little litigants can sue when they don't find a toy in their box of Cracker Jack?

I really don't mean to trivialize a serious question, and finally we will do whatever the Senate wants to do about a local teaching award, but can we not define ourselves—in fact, may already have done so—in ways which incorporate what is best in the idea of a teaching award and recognize the other dimensions of our professional activity as well. Moreover, harking back to what I implied a bit earlier about those who might want to define our mission in a way that would eliminate or reduce the support we can give to discipline-oriented research, the time may not be in joint.

I'm not certain what may have been heartening or disheartening in these brief reflections about some of our present condition in this more-than-ordinarily-parlous time for higher education. Our present estate, good and bad, might be metaphorized as Shakespeare did life itself when he called it a "web . . . of a mingled yarn." Even if dark threads are dominant in the immediate prospect, our cheerfulness about higher education can be vindicated by seeing it as derivative from the larger Biblical vision which proclaims faith as the substance of things hoped for, the evidence of things not seen. I'll put my long-range bets on Montaigne. But until we at least get our library, Larry Clipper—who will be shocked to hear I *might* agree with him—*may* have a point too.

Warm welcome, good colleagues old and new, to 1982-83 and what I trust will be many other happy years ahead.

Like Grim Death
Delivered at the Fall Faculty Meeting, September 2, 1983

Anecdotes of education surround with wit and insight the honoring of the core value of curiosity, even obscure inquiry, in the university, while affirming social and economic responsibility in a time of enrollment decline and constricted budget.

On this occasion two years ago I spoke of Olga Perschbacher, a superb teacher who had significant influence on the lives of those of us fortunate enough to have had her as our instructor in high school senior English. Now in speaking of H. T. Price, my tutor in the English honors program during my senior year in college, when I tell you the "H. T." stood for "Hereward Thimbleby," one might bemoan the rarity today of such wonderful names as those in Dickens or Thackeray which at the same time identify and characterize: Mr. Pecksniff, Lord Huddleston Fuddleston, Lady Jane Sheepshanks.

On first impression, Professor Price seemed a Thimbleby indeed. His manner and speech were hesitant—almost halting. He forgot appointments as in his spare hours he worked on the Middle English Dictionary—now some fifty years after its inception published halfway through the letter P. He fell into bushes when he leaned forward to smell the flowers; he thought bright green ties were the mark of truly sensitive persons. By all the text-book criteria of what makes for effective teaching, he would have to be judged a failure. I first came to know him in my sophomore year when I enrolled in his course on Shakespeare's tragedies. We read a play a week, each one as he assigned it being introduced as "the greatest play Shakespeare ever wrote." He would never give us any direction except to say we should look for the central theme in each work and then decide how every character, every scene, every line related to that theme—establishing it, developing it, embellishing it. He rarely lectured. Instead, he would have us open our texts, indicate a passage, and ask us to make the appropriate linkages—backward and forward, inside and out, upside and down—to the theme. If too many of us were inept (as we often were) he would dismiss us, not unkindly, saying that we should go home to read more closely and reflect more carefully.

His method, or lack of it if you will, was a triumph of substance over procedure. He was born on Madagascar of English parents, educated at Oxford and at Bonn, impressed into the German army during World War I and fought the Russians, for whom he developed a somewhat irrational inveterate distrust. His cosmopolitan background may have caused him to care deeply about the broad human scene, and although he was thoroughly trained in the tradition of Germanic scholarship, he was never pedantic.

As you might have guessed, his students—or at least the better ones—loved him, and when he retired we did what he said we did in the prefatory note to the little book I now hold up before you (*Construction in Shakespeare*, The University of Michigan Contributions in Modern Philology, Number 17, May, 1951):

> On the occasion of my retirement in the summer of 1949 my students collected a fund to be appropriated for a lecture to be given by me at the University of Michigan and afterwards to be published. I now present to them their lecture in print with the addition of some matter which pressure of time compelled me to omit when it was delivered. In gratitude for their gratitude I should like to dedicate this booklet to them, but then it is already just as much their work as mine.

Those words were typical of his unfailingly gracious spirit, a spirit vexed mainly by the generations of critics who argued that while Shakespeare wrote fine poetry and created some unforgettable characters, he didn't know how to write a play, that he was deficient in construction—observing neither the traditional Aristotelian unities nor more modern canons of how a well-made drama should be put together. In brief, his unswerving position was that each play created its own organic, as opposed to merely mechanical, form.

In his retirement lecture, as Professor Price touched upon several of Shakespeare's works, he cited with obvious approval W. Somerset Maugham's maxim about essential coherence: "... in a story as in a play, you must make up your mind what your point is and stick to it like grim death." His ranging presentation concluded with his judgment that to "... divorce any beauty of Shakespeare from his construction (that is, his form, his ordered development of an idea) is to be blind to the greatest of his beauties. Of Shakespeare it is preeminently true: 'Order the beauty of all beauty is.'"

Your having indulged me in this reminiscence, let me make a leap reflecting now on a mastering idea about higher education that should be asserted far more often than it is and tenaciously clung to like grim death. A spate of recent reports show that critics are not wanting who find all of our educational system in disarray. For example, *A Nation at Risk: The Imperative for Educational Reform*, at Secretary Bell's direction published a little while back by the National Commission on Excellence in Education, deplores the softening of the curriculum which has caused test scores to drop and America to fall behind other industrialized nations in technical and scientific productivity. The colleges, at least by implication, are excoriated for their inadequate training of teachers, and for their diffuseness of motive.

On another front, and with a different emphasis, George Weathersby, who recently resigned as Indiana's Commissioner for Higher Education, has indicted universities for being out of step with society at large, for preserving a status quo which serves the too-limited interests of the faculty to the neglect and detriment of students and the public at large.

This is not the place to dispute some of the tone and the findings of the Bell Commission, though a basic fault I think is that it does not adequately recognize or acknowledge the stupendous job of general acculturation which the public schools have been called upon to do, a job—given its magnitude—they have done quite well. But if the report has the effect of galvanizing national attention to the need for greater rigor at all levels in the study of verbal and mathematical symbols, it will have had all the justification it needs.

Dr. Weathersby's critique is quite another matter. In arguing that higher education is "vulnerable to competition from others who offer services that are more market-sensitive (and have a labor structure that is less restrictive)," he is faithful to his consistent view that colleges should be purveyors of whatever abets society in obtaining the various goods it allegedly needs. "Need," so far as I can tell, appears to be synonymous with "want," and I would guess that in impugning the relevance to serious concerns of faculty interests, George would be most sympathetic to Senator Proxmire and his Golden Fleece awards.

Let us concede what might be worst cases. I cite one instance from fact, one from fiction.

In September, 1940, an article entitled "Beowulf's Arm-Lock," by Calvin S. Brown, Jr. of the University of Georgia appeared in *PMLA*, the prestigious scholarly journal devoted to language and literature. In seven large pages, it analyzes a short passage in the Anglo-Saxon epic *Beowulf*, taking great pains to explain how, in the light of modern wrestling technique, Beowulf was able to tear off the arm of the monster Grendel.

When I first read the piece, I thought it might be a parody. It isn't, even though *The New Yorker* could well publish its opening sentence under the label "Disappointments We Never Felt." That sentence goes: "Many readers of *Beowulf* must have felt that its first climax, the fight with Grendel, is something of a disappointment."

The example from fiction comes from Kingsley Amis's novel, *Lucky Jim*, when the hero, Jim Dixon, faces a moment of truth as his superior, Professor Welch, asks him the exact title of an article that must be placed for Jim to insure his reappointment and advance his professional prospects. Jim is dismayed at the need to recite the soul-dampening title, and these thoughts go through his head:

> It was a perfect title, in that it crystallized the article's niggling mindlessness, its funereal parade of yawn-enforcing facts, the pseudo-light it threw upon non-problems. Dixon had read, or begun to read, dozens like it, but his own seemed worse than most in its air of being convinced of its own usefulness and

significance. "In considering this strangely neglected topic," it began. This what neglected topic? This strangely what topic? This strangely neglected what? His thinking all this without having defiled and set fire to the typescript only made him appear to himself as more of a hypocrite and fool. "Let's see," he echoed Welch in a pretended effort of memory: "oh, yes; *The Economic Influence of the Developments in Ship Building Techniques, 1450 to 1485....*"

Such researches may seem more useless than Colonel Stoopnagle's invention of ten foot poles that nobody would touch anybody with, or Ralph Kramden's get-rich-quick plan to concoct calorie-less pizza. In that vein, are students in introductory or even advanced poetry classes deprived if the instructor doesn't mention synecdoche and metonymy, let alone anacrusis and catalexis? Isn't it enough if they appreciate the metaphoric principle and the metaphor for metaphor which defines it as a cocktail of the spheres? Or is even that too much to excite the interest of any sane, pragmatic person—the person who pays taxes to support IU? What bread does such knowledge bake, what "need" does it serve?

It is cheaply easy to deride the seemingly impractical, trivial, and hair-splitting inquiries made by certain inquisitive types, but it is far better that the play and exercise of mind be given the broadest possible scope than that there be prior restrictive definitions of what is "needed" or what is "useful." The world obviously does not have crying desire for a raft of catalexis experts, but it would be a much poorer place if a person were not allowed to choose to be one, and if he or she should be told that a natural habitat for such a grazing mind is not first and foremost the university. The same for people who are interested in Beowulf's arm-lock on Grendel, or for those who have an authentic concern for the economic influence of ship building techniques from 1450 to 1485. King Lear had it right:

> Oh, reason not the need. Our basest beggars
> Are in the poorest thing superfluous.
> Allow not nature more than nature needs,
> Man's life's as cheap as beast's.

If the ordinary, or even less than ordinary, run of scholarship and experimentation represents the honorable human desire to satisfy curiosity, to seek connections, to find cause and effect, how the much more worthy of support are those towering achievements in the laboratory, the studio, and the library produced by the most gifted of our colleagues throughout the academic community.

Practically, what is the bearing of all this on our condition at IUSB as the 1983-84 academic year begins? We have come off a difficult 1982-83, when mainly as a result of diminished appropriations and a two-year decline in enrollment we were obliged to reduce our operating base by $400,000. Through everyone's forbearance we were able to keep to a minimum the number of persons actually affected. I do not think there will be a need for further systematic reduction in the foreseeable future, although there will be pressures to reallocate funds internally, about which I will say more in a few minutes.

As to new programs, we have the computer science degree on track, and unless some unanticipated hitch occurs, a week from today the appropriate authorizations should be given so that by next fall we will have in South Bend the ten-year-sought-for first engineering technology associate degree. Contractual details remain to be worked out with Purdue, but managerial niceties are less important than that the curriculum be here to serve a genuine regional need.

Without reference to specific program, studies are under way in Elkhart which very likely will demonstrate that more offerings are needed there. And despite random speculation as to the source of those offerings, it is absurd to think that anyone other than IUSB should play the leading, if not the sole, part.

I know that some months ago I promised I wouldn't say anything more about the library until I had something specific to report. I have nothing specific to report, but our shared frustration is so great that its public airing might offer some relief. Should the two-year clock be started? What consequences would ensue from such a move? Recall one of Walter Mitty's fantasies of heroism when he was placed against the wall to be executed and, in a last defiant gesture, held up his hand saying, "To hell with the blindfold." The flip side of that, of course, is that the mundane Walter would meekly accept the blindfold because he wouldn't want to make trouble. James Thurber, where are you now when we need you?

I have written to President Ryan and Executive Vice President Pinnell (who is also now the new President of the IU Foundation) that it is impossible to rank order the things we would hope to receive from a capital campaign until we know whether or not a library will be part of the consideration. But both in the detail of special drives and in anticipation of enhanced annual giving, our prospects will be improved by the appointment I expect to make in the next six weeks or so of a person to succeed Walt Collins. After three rounds of preliminary screening, the candidates to be interviewed will have been identified by September 26, on which date the Newsletter will also list the members of two new internal committees, one to provide our link with the activities of Project Future (on whose Board of Trustees I now sit), and the other to work with Walt's successor, with me, and an activated IUSB Foundation Board in advancing the cause of our campus in seeking private support such as we were delighted to receive recently from The Bendix Corporation to assist in our computer program.

Nonetheless, even as we continue to respond to market need in program development, and rightly contribute our expertise to the general economic development of our community, hark back to the ineluctable idea of what must always be at the center of our concern—that as a university we deal centrally and always with things in their intellectual and aesthetic formulation. As antitheses, consider first the IBM radio ad in which an uneducated but subliminally erotic female voice informs us that there is no fun like the fun to be had in fooling around with computers. Clearly, all that has a great deal to do with sales but nothing at all to do with an understanding of binary mathematics or the properties of electricity which make computer science possible and intelligible. In contrast, Otis Romine a short time back told an IU golf outing that as a necessary antidote to the excesses of talk about high tech and bottom lines, we should think more about low tech and top lines. Robert Frost, I think it was, who said with similar metaphoric meaning that we should be more concerned with insight than sight, essence than sense, metaphysics than physics.

The top line for IU as a system, for our IUSB, and for all good colleges and universities is how to keep alive those indispensable disciplines which are the witness of our essential humanity. In the matter of internal reallocation, do we bend totally to what is immediately wanted, or do we muster all the strength we have to say that philosophy must be supported, literature, music, art, drama, true scientific inquiry—all those things which may not be currently popular as measured by numbers but—hucksterish Salvationists and commercialists to the contrary—offer the best chance for humankind not only to survive but to flourish.

Last October, at the local United Nations dinner, Father Hesburgh spoke of kooks who write him saying that the nuclear threat is really a blessing. Let it come down so that the "unco' guid" Bobby Burns writes about can be saved and all the wicked eternally damned. Father Ted said it might be that God has reason enough to destroy mankind, but he was sure that God didn't want us to make the decision.

In our institutional commitment to keeping the intellectual tradition alive, what do we do? What is just? If declining or continuously feeble enrollments in key disciplines persist, what strategies will sustain majors and elective options until a hoped for better day dawns? One aid is to recognize that there are many adults with bachelor's degrees in our community, mature and experientially wise, not interested in college because they think it will help their economic well-being, but because they would like to learn further, and receive the not ignoble insignia of an advanced degree. The proposals already in process in arts and sciences for a generalized master's degree should be brought to a resolution as soon as possible so that a combination of 300-level courses and selected old and new 500-level courses will constitute a most reputable program I can present with full confidence to Dean Solt of the Graduate School and other officers whose approval we will need to have.

Can we not also support small classes by even more flexible definitions than we have now of what comprises a reasonable teaching assignment, not only as to class size within individual departments and divisions but among them all collectively? And true to the notion that we should try harder to lead market rather than simply respond to it, what greater equity can we achieve in compensation among the various disciplines, in the assignment of summer teaching, in setting adjunct rates?

Kent Laudeman was one of the main architects last year in a survey our Alumni Office and University Relations made of all 1972 and 1977 IUSB graduates—those who had been out ten years and five years, respectively. Nearly 40% responded to a series of questions as to how IUSB had helped their lives and careers. The responses were almost uniformly positive. That did not surprise us, and it is you sitting here today or your colleagues in kind who account for it. Our record in scholarship and creativity has impressed every reviewing body which has visited us these past several years. Relative to our numbers, we continue to have the best record of any of IU's eight campuses in the attainment of all-University distinguished teaching awards, and I think at last we are reaching agreement on how we can annually give local recognition which will also represent our entry into system-wide deliberations. This fall we will obtain a plaque (not a plague as a great misprint once called it) to list all of our past honorees and those yet to come.

Your concern for quality—the new curriculum in arts and sciences, the strengthened requirements for entry into the business major, the competency in composition testing for some time now done by the Division of Education: all these representative instances of the vitality and serious intent of this faculty make IUSB better and stronger with each passing year.

And now, at the risk of sounding like Thurber's young man who cried "Excelsior!" let me say unabashedly what a great bunch of people you are, and how happy I am to serve with you in advancing the welfare of this campus and the distinguished University of which we are an integral and truly considerable part.

Touchstones
Delivered at the Fall Faculty Meeting,
September 7, 1984

*Invoking a sense of the secular and sacred spirit in education, this excerpt
celebrates significant markers in IUSB's growth: budget stability, and
engineering curriculum (Purdue-linked), expanded programs in Elkhart
County, possession within months of the Associates "cheese factory," an
improved fund-raising program, and a library looming large on the near
horizon.*

. . .

So much for the time being about some of the present facts of our
situation. Let me turn in what remains to matters unequivocally
positive. A few minutes ago Dean Harriman unveiled the plaque
promised last fall, ocular proof of our fidelity to our students. On it are
inscribed the names of the twelve IUSB faculty members who have
won all-University teaching awards in the past thirteen years—a number greater than that won by the five other smaller campuses.

That distinction was gained not by any sacrifice of our insistence on
research, creative activity, and wide-ranging service to the University,
to the region, and in many instances to the state and nation. What has
motivated this faculty, in the two decades that I have been privileged
to observe it, is the recognition that we have not so much chosen our
vocation, as in the old, honorable sense of "calling," been chosen for it.

For ours indeed is a noble profession. Even though the flat, pragmatic language of agencies, commissions, and public spokesmen often
means well, it trivializes the high seriousness of what teaching and
learning are finally all about. Analogy might be drawn with what

Matthew Arnold said about much of the verse of the eighteenth century in comparison with those passages in which the true accent of
poetic insight is gloriously sounded—passages which he called "touch-
stones." For example, Dryden's "A milk-white Hind, immortal and
unchanged,/ Fed on the leaves and in the forest ranged" or Pope's "To
Hounslow Heath I point, and Banstead Down;/Thence comes your
mutton, and these chicks my own" as compared with Shakespeare's
"If thou didst ever hold me in thy heart,/Absent thee from felicity

Lester Wolfson and Eileen Bender (English) 4/25/1988,
at the installation of his successor, Daniel Cohen.

awhile,/And in this harsh world draw thy breath in pain/To tell my
story . . ."

Compare the language of any official report (it is too distressing
to give examples) with the vatic eloquence often present in books like
Jacques Barzun's *Teacher in America*, Mark Van Doren's *Liberal Education*, Gilbert Highet's *The Art of Teaching*, or that perennial guide,
Newman's *The Idea of a University*:

> . . . a University training is the great ordinary means to a great
> but ordinary end; it aims at raising the intellectual tone of
> society, at cultivating the public mind, at purifying the nation-
> al taste, at supplying true principles to popular enthusiasm
> and fixed aims to popular aspiration, at giving enlargement

and sobriety to the ideas of the age, at facilitating the exercise
of political power, and refining the intercourse of private life.

Twenty years ago, in the first of these annual remarks, I ventured
to say to a full-time total staff one-seventh the size of what it is today
that although we are a secular institution, we have a sacred charge . . .
that we are really concerned with something quite different from the
quantitative. I went on to say that whatever our particular discipline,
our passion for intellectual order is akin to all other concerns for the
spirit, and ended by quoting in their entirety Stephen Spender's soar-
ing lines beginning "I think continually of those who were truly great,"
and ending "Born of the sun they traveled a short while towards the
sun,/And left the vivid air signed with their honor."

In like vein, now twenty years later, I read another poem which
expresses how literature and the arts (and true science as well) can
rescue us from the thrall of our unreflecting responses to mundane
existence typically apprehended. John Updike's "The Angels," its
entreated thrones being the order of angels third closest to God in
the celestial hierarchy, speaks to that sense of the awesomely blended
secular and sacred which, whatever our personal hope of heaven, sound
education so beautifully provides:

> They are above us all the time,
> The good gentlemen, Mozart and Bach,
> Scarlatti and Handel and Brahms,
> lavishing measures of light down upon us,
> telling us, over and over, there is a realm
> above this plane of silent compromise.
> They are around us everywhere, the old seers,
> Matisse and Vermeer, Cezanne and Piero,
> greeting us echoing in subway tunnels,
> springing like winter flowers from postcards
> Scotch-taped to white kitchen walls,
> waiting larger than life in shadowy galleries
> to whisper that edges of color
> lie all about us innocent as grass.
> They are behind us, beneath us,

the abysmal books, Shakespeare and Tolstoy,
the Bible and Proust and Cervantes,
burning in memory like leaky furnace doors,
minepits of honesty from which we escaped
with dilated suspicions. Love us, dead thrones,
sing us to sleep, awaken our eyes,
comfort with terror our mortal afternoons.

Warm welcome once again, good colleagues old and new. May it be
a satisfying year for us all.

Chocolates, Allbran,
and Asymptotes

Delivered at the Fall Faculty Meeting,
September 5, 1986

Speaking at the outset of his final year, Wolfson notes the imminent ground-breaking for the library, as well as the recent trustee approval for the first Master of Liberal Studies degree in the IU system. Such great events mark the asymptotic movement of the university toward its "ideally beckoning but ever-receding goal."

If nothing else should prove memorable about these remarks, I hope that at least the title has piqued your curiosity. I'm not going to explain it until near the very end, but the mathematicians have probably already guessed that "asymptotes" will not be used literally. Moreover, "chocolates" and "Allbran" have nothing to do with current discussion about nutrition or the value of fiber in the diet. And while the suspense may be no greater than that created by the legended bad actor whose emotions ran the gamut from A to B, bear with it while I report briefly on a number of good things as the 1986-87 academic year commences.

Surpassing every other development is the prospective ground-breaking for the Franklin D. Schurz library. I hold before you the huge, to-our-spirit many-splendored volume of specifications drawn up by Edward Larrabee Barnes Associates and Cole Associates as answer to the fear that we would never see this happy day. And despite what you may have read in the *South Bend Tribune* this late summer, the necessary $2,000,000 in private funding will indeed be in hand, and the first shovel of dirt should be turned before the snow flies.

More immediately, during the past year we have converted part of the University Center into a long-sought on-campus child-care facility, and soon improved cooperative effort between Student Services and the program in Counseling and Guidance will be signaled by an open house in a remodeled portion of the Administration Building. Tomorrow I will be in Indianapolis where the Trustees are expected to approve a lease for an Elkhart office and the first phase in the transformation of the "cheese factory" into a fine arts building, where we at last can offer under one roof all our studio instruction in that great expressive discipline.

1986 – soon to house the Fine Arts studios and offices

Funding for the conversion will come from savings in the cost of rented space and reserves that have been accumulated in various of our auxiliary enterprises. A recreation building for IUSB will not be part of the University's capital request for the 1987-89 biennium, but I am confident that it—along with a green mall from the library to Mishawaka Avenue and a building for technology—will be part of our inventory well before the arrival of the millennium.

As to curriculum, a most significant advance—not only for our campus but for the entire University—is the Trustee approval we have to offer a master of liberal studies degree. The Commission for Higher Education must still give assent, but that should come in due course. Last spring, Les Lamon, John Lewis, and I made two appearances before the Graduate School Council and gained their enthusiastic endorsement of the first truly inter-disciplinary arts and sciences master's degree to be offered in the Indiana University system—a consummation devoutly to be wished if higher education is to continue to reflect its highest mission of advocacy for the intrinsic value of knowledge and generalized intelligence.

While the liberal studies degree can be offered without much added cost, there *are* several repeated and new budgetary initiatives in the University's 1987-89 operating request. My second and last show-and-tell item is this copy of the total system request that I now hold up before you. In his address last Tuesday, President Ryan spoke of several aspects of that request, and since his speech will soon be printed in the *IU Newspaper*, I will not give any detail here other than to say that we are seeking funds for a statewide MBA program which may in time replace the present MSBA; that we hope to offer a complete generic BSN program in nursing; and that a systemic approach has been taken to the need for equipment in the biological sciences on every one of the University's eight campuses. If that approach is successful, other departments and divisions should in time benefit in a similar way.

Since it has long been our practice and policy at IUSB to share every detail relating to the budget, the Academic Senate and any of its relevant committees is always welcome to ask questions of me and to examine the request that President Ryan and others of us will be explaining to, and defending before, members of the General Assembly both in the months just ahead and after formal convening of the Assembly in January.

By now, most of you know that this will be President Ryan's last year in office, as on June 13 he announced his intention to relinquish his post not later than September 1, 1987. For two and a half years as vice president and chancellor for regional campuses, and now for fifteen and a half years as president, he has worked tirelessly to narrow the dollar gap in state support behind each comparable credit hour no matter where it might be taken. Only those few who have been relatively close to him can even remotely appreciate the tremendous tugs and pulls exerted on one who must attempt to satisfy a diverse constituency of eight campuses, three thousand full-time faculty, over fourteen thousand full-time employees, and nearly eighty thousand students—not to mention alumni and 150 legislators. Others will chronicle in other places the many achievements of the Ryan presidency. I mention here only his unswerving attention to international co-operation and understanding, an echo of which has recently reached IUSB in our having six of our faculty early participants in the Malaysia program, and in our having just established an office for international students directed by Romesh Mehra.

But even as officers and faculty and students arrive and depart in the 350-year-old American college and university academic procession, what abides?

A standard sentence in our annual commencement exercises reads: "Most importantly, we recognize knowledge itself as the fountainhead of liberating ideas and the source of society's hope for improvement." Clarity and depth of understanding, refinement and sensitivity of feeling, responsiveness to the symbols which make us human—*these* are the ends all education seeks, no matter what its temporal permutations.

Now let me take up, in reverse order, each of the three words in the title of these remarks.

In mathematics, an asymptote is a straight line associated with a curve such that as a point P moves out along an infinite branch of the curve the distance from the point P to the line approaches zero and the slope of the curve at P approaches the slope of the line. In short, the line and the curve move toward coincidence but never totally achieve it. Analogizing the movement of P to the development of intellectual awareness, and the unending end of the line to total awareness, it can be argued that good instruction moves understanding toward an ideally beckoning but ever-receding goal.

If all that is too ponderous to merit pondering, come at the question of good teaching and learning by way of a parody. Many of you may have read Kahlil Gibran's *The Prophet*, where the master speaks—often in sententious Biblical-Blakean prose—of Love, Marriage, Laws, Freedom, Pain, Time, Reason and Passion, Good and Evil, Pleasure, Beauty,

Religion, Death, etc., etc. Some years ago a wit calling himself Kellogg Allbran wrote a book entitled *The Profit*, in which a guru expostulates on all the big topics. He pontificates: "No man is worth more than any other man, and no man is worth more than $1.98." When a disciple asks him to speak of Fate, he discourses on gross tonnage, on sidings, on loadings and unloadings. The puzzled novice suggests that the master is speaking about Freight, to which the zanily antic, ever-upbeat guru responds that "Freight is good too."

The master asks the disciple to name the brightness of the illumination which constitutes Enlightenment. "Is it like the light of a thousand stars?" "Brighter." "A million stars?" "Brighter." "A billion stars?" "Brighter." "I give up." "You shouldn't have quit—you were getting close." Where should we stop in what we expect of our students and ourselves?

As a last instance, I cite C. S. Lewis, who in his book *Miracles* works a delightful variant on the sophisticated religious belief that even a Dante can convey only the dimmest tracings of what the joys of heaven or the pains of hell are really like.

Lewis speculates that a limited view of beatitude and transfiguration is "like that of a small boy who, on being told that the sexual act was the highest bodily pleasure, should immediately ask whether you ate chocolates at the same time. On receiving the answer 'No,' he might regard absence of chocolates as the chief characteristic of sexuality. In vain would you tell him that the reason why lovers in their carnal raptures don't bother about chocolates is that they have something better to think of. The boy knows chocolate: he does not know the positive thing that excludes it."

And so, until sound education rescues us, we remain frozen within the limits of misplaced certain certainties. Last Saturday, after listening to the sumptuous musical glory of Richard Strauss's *Der Rosenkavalier*, for the thousandth time I could not comprehend the popularity of an abomination called MTV, or the caterwauling reminiscent of the bad orchestra in Joseph Conrad's *Victory* that not so much made music as murdered silence.

In closing, I reflect on an IUSB student who was a modest epitome of that asymptotic P, of dawning enlightenment, of awareness that goes way beyond the satisfaction experienced by the most confirmed chocoholics.

On May 7, 1985, a 61 year-old woman who had started college at Tufts University in 1941 received her Bachelor of General Studies degree as a member of our nineteenth graduating class. She served as treasurer of the 1985 Student Alumni Council, had been president of the Ancilla College Alumni Association, and was a blessing to all who knew her.

A few weeks ago Winnie Brown died unexpectedly only hours before her son's wedding. The ceremony went on because that is what she would have wished. Last Sunday I attended her memorial service at the Wesley United Methodist Church in Culver. The minister and two eulogists, faithful to their faith, spoke of her having completed that road all runners come, and trusted in that haven where all losses are restored and sorrows end.

Ted Hengesbach, I, and many others here loved her as one who helped us to help her in gaining such understanding as it is the University's privilege to impart. Winnie believed, with us, that the University is—or should be—not a microcosm of the larger world but rather a paradigm of what that world might become.

Welcome, good colleagues all, to the year we now begin.

The Wolfson Papers

Literature and Humanities
Addresses

An Existentialist View of Research
Delivered at a convention of the Speech Association of the Eastern States, Henry Hudson Hotel, New York, April 8, 1960

Both science and commerce would reduce humans to quantifiable, manipulable objects. In the academy, the ambition for rational, systemic order and the consequent pressure for faculty to win tenure, raises, and promotions have fueled the engine of research and publication. Instead, intellectual curiosity and a passion for humanity's profound predicaments should propel our efforts to understand and to articulate that understanding.

Early in his novel, *Lucky Jim*, Kingsley Amis presents the hero, Jim Dixon, facing a moment of truth when his superior, Professor Welch, asks him the exact title of an article that must be placed for Jim to insure his reappointment and advance his professional prospects. Jim is dismayed at the need to recite the soul-dampening title, and these thoughts go through his head:

> It was a perfect title, in that it crystallized the article's niggling mindlessness, its funereal parade of yawn-enforcing facts, the pseudo-light it threw upon non-problems. Dixon had read, or begun to read, dozens like it, but his own seemed worse than most in its air of being convinced of its own usefulness and significance. "In considering this strangely neglected topic," it began. This what neglected topic? This strangely what topic? This strangely neglected what? His thinking all this without having defiled and set fire to the typescript only made him appear to himself as

more of a hypocrite and fool. "Let's see," he echoed Welch in a pretended effort of memory: "oh, yes; *The economic influence of the developments in ship building techniques*, 1450 to 1485. . . ."

A bit later, when Professor Welch suggests that it is virtually impossible to know what any article is worth unless a learned journal accepts it, Dixon thought that

> on the contrary, he had a good idea of what his article was worth from several points of view. From one of these, the thing's worth could be expressed in one short hyphenated indecency; from another, it was worth the amount of frenzied fact-grubbing and fanatical boredom that had gone into it; from yet another, it was worthy of its aim, the removal of the "bad impression" he'd so far made in the college and in his department.

Now consider the passage in Soren Kierkegaard's *Concluding Unscientific Postscript* in which the pseudonymous author, Johannes Climacus, describes how he became a writer. After ten years as a haphazard student, reading and thinking idly, it dawned on him that his contemporaries had been developing metaphysical systems and creating inventions which allegedly benefited mankind by making life easier. It occurred to Johannes that he might aid men by making things harder, because they would be more honestly seen; that, at a banquet where men have overeaten, the truly helpful person is the one who brings the vomitive to purge the surfeit.

A third, and last, bit of introductory material: in his book, *An Introduction to Research in Speech*, Professor J. Jeffrey Auer, in discussing motivations for undertaking research projects, puts last in a list of decreasing laudability "such basic motivations as satisfying research degree requirements, or undertaking a project that may be publishable."

The remainder of this paper will be concerned with exploring, from an existentialist point of view, some of the implications for research of the bearings in the three sources just cited. It may be that

I have imperfectly formulated or irresponsibly conceived some of the queries and suggestions which follow, but I firmly believe that some of the emphases of existentialist thought—provocatively heretical as they are—can help give stronger foundation and more vital results to studies in speech, literature, and the other humanities.

A complete answer to the question, what is existentialism? may possibly be given only by professional philosophers, and undeniably many of the existentialist's key terms—being, anxiety, freedom, authenticity, transcendence, existence, despair, encounter, and nothingness—require a comprehension of their technical meanings before a layman can use them confidently. However, despite complexities and the differences among various existentialist philosophers and theologians, certain common directions in the existentialist analysis of knowledge and of what it means to be a human being can be clearly discerned and, if we are convinced, then applied to the kind of life and career we choose to make for ourselves.

The fundamental charge of existentialism against Platonic-Hegelian types of philosophic structures is that such structures are predominantly or exclusively rationalistic, and ignore, obscure, or explain away men's individual and personal feelings of what it means to live, to suffer, to enjoy, and to die. Against systems which elevate intellect and deny the passions, and against any form of natural, social, or psychological determinism which reduces man to a resultant of forces working on him, existentialism asserts man's need and power to make himself uniquely human. Traditional philosophic and scientific views in various ways treat men as things rather than as persons who through their autonomous choices determine what and that they shall *be*.

Some consequences of non-existential modes of thinking are the perversities of pride and power that typify modern man's acquisitive and belligerent temper. At a feeble best, man viewed as a consuming thing leads to the pallid, faceless anonymity of contemporary mass society.

The existentialist views man's deepest feelings as phenomenological wholes, not be reduced by any method which removes man himself from the center of being and as the key to being. He rebels in particular against our elevating of partial and imperfect symbolic methods into privileged positions, particularly the method of exact science.

While our addiction to the siren-songs of modern advertising should disabuse us of the idea that, in any final sense, we are a scientific people, and though in recent years there have been many evidences of anti-intellectualism, we have largely put our faith in certain limited ideals of adjustment and in the "more and better things for better living" afforded by modern technology. "Knowledge," for most men, thus becomes identified with whatever enables prediction and manipulation of behavior, or production and use of material goods. Such knowledge depends ultimately on the application of mathematical and scientific symbols to the solution of prescribed problems, and basic research is justified in the public mind in the hope that it will have practical consequences for an acquisitive and power-oriented society.

Unhappily, whatever motives prompt an interest in science, its theoretical and practical triumphs have served to devalue, in subtle ways, literature, the arts, and the immediacies of human communication in the personal interchange of formal and informal speaking. Most damaging is the belief that causal-genetic explanations set the limits to what can be truly called "knowledge," are in fact equivalent to knowledge. Man, as well as the world, becomes an object to be categorized into various systems, but always systems which allow no intrinsic meaning to our immediately felt experience as thinking, feeling, willing, doing consciousnesses. Such awareness is reduced to "mere feeling," many modern semanticists apparently considering the affective dimension of language a subsidiary, if important, adjunct to the denotative and practical. Bertrand Russell states that "whatever can be known, can be known by means of science; but matters which are legitimately matters of feeling lie outside its province." Though Russell does not intend to derogate feeling, in fact he does so by making it "unknowable" and allowing it no ingress to knowledge.

The existentialist view is that reality is much broader, and fundamentally of different character, than what is expressed by the symbolic statements of quantitative relationship in the formulas and pointer readings of modern science. What we know scientifically we know, in Kurt Riezler's phrase, as "Anonymous Observers"—by one capacity of our minds only, stripped so far as possible of any irrelevances of inward feeling, the qualitative pressure of joy or love or fright or aesthetic response in immediate encounter.

As early as this, it may be clear that insofar as studies in the humanities have patterned themselves after scientific models, the existentialist will protest that historical accounts of the methods and effects of this speaker or that speaker on a given occasion are either worthless or pernicious unless the researcher evaluates his discoveries by an authentic norm which, so far as can be done, judges the motives of both the speaker and his audience. History is not simply a body of inert facts to be garnered by a dispassionate observer. To the existentialist, history is always history-for-me: I am engulfed in it, and the "for-me" implies valuation of meanings. Science cannot give evaluative norms, but existentialism, insisting upon the need for exercising ethical judgment, would make short shrift of Plato's old problem in the *Gorgias* and the *Phaedrus* as to whether the rhetorician need be merely one skilled in devices, or whether he should be also a responsible human being.

In descriptive and experimental studies, as well as in historical, the researcher should always be honestly convinced that what he is attempting will help develop his own freedom as a responsible human agent, making the endless effort to break through the mold of pattern and role-defined expectation. If he chooses authentically for himself, he will be choosing what has possible meaning for all men. The Dale Carnegie "tested and proven" techniques, or the methods of many approaches to business and professional speech, with their false generating of a hollow cheeriness, and their implicit view of human beings as instruments to be used or objects to be worked on, violate the genuinely human. Research studies which contribute to such goals and methods are likewise anti-human.

Speech as a field is concerned with the total act and art of oral communication. In practice, apart from the clinical aspects of speech and hearing therapy, this has meant attention to the practical problems of decision-making and policy-implementing through discussion, debate, and public address. Predominantly aesthetic, as opposed to practical, matters have been the province of theater and oral interpretation.

The great unifying strand running through both practical and aesthetic concerns is rhetoric, with its attention to ultimate problems of oral intent, method, and effectiveness. Rhetoric has always worked in close league with, and appropriated for its own uses, the relevant insights of philosophy and psychology. In many ways, then, speech broadly conceived is the fundamental human discipline. The existentialist believes that we become uniquely human by the skill with which our total psyches create, use, and respond to symbols—words, gestures, formulas, lines, colors, musical notes, ritual enactments. But the word, and connected discourse, is probably the most indispensable of all symbols. And the possibility of my openness to others is created by the responsibility with which I use words: "Speak, that I may know thee." Thus, any trivializing, cheapening, or opportunistic use of language is especially reprehensible.

Unfortunately, though a great scientist's passion for intellectual order represents a valid human choice, adopting scientific models for alleged humanistic research has led to a proliferation of studies in which data are accumulated apparently for their own, or more honorifically, "for truth's sake." But scientific notions of truth are complexly inapplicable to my responses to other people and to the world into which I am thrown. In such responses, a more meaningful criterion than "fact" or "truth" is "fittingness." When I come to terms with my own unmasked experience, or when I relate to others in loving encounter, I have a feeling of "rightness" or "fittingness" which cannot be quantified or reduced. In many traditional patterns of scholarly investigation, we have, as Nietzsche indicated, no genuine sense of our own activities; we have become mere thinking machines. But if we are humans, and not machines, we can never conceive of communication, oral or written, as a means to power rather than to authentic interchange, nor can we conceive of it as a counter in a game we play called "Scholarship."

Nothing can be more absurd than the notion that all actual and incipient college teachers, particularly teachers of speech or English, should have on tap an endless stream of ideas that can be turned into published research. Yet teachers at every school of any pretension will recognize this adaptation of Dr. Johnson's remark, "Patriotism is the last refuge of a scoundrel": "To claim to rest content in being a good teacher is the last refuge of a failure." Like the world of mass man which it presumably stands against, the university itself is often guilty of judging by labels rather than by any willingness, or perhaps ability, to make genuine assessments. A man of rich and comprehensive mind—but without the stipulated degrees—almost always ranks lower on the academic ladder than one who has the proper stamps. And despite frequent administrative protest to the contrary, the man whose bibliography is regular and long almost always ranks higher than the man who believes that the time he spends reading books of major import will be more beneficial to him and everyone else than equivalent time spent on things he himself might write.

Needless to say, rationalization is always a danger here, and few claims are more irritating than those of inept teachers who think their inability in and disinclination to scholarship are nothing inherent but simply a matter of their having chosen to be the fine teachers they imagine they are.

Thus, in many ways, the university community, which has a moral obligation to be moral as well as intelligent, is frequently riddled by the vices of an inauthentic playing of parts, and of an irresponsible distortion of values based on a misleading notion of what knowledge and success are. Young disciplines, like speech, in their desire to strengthen their academic repute frequently ape the worst faults of other subjects hag-ridden by the mania for fact-digging in the empty pretense that something new will be added to knowledge. The truth is that few men are gifted with the ability to say anything new of consequence in the humanities, or to comment with honestly publishable originality on what has been said or written in the past. Yet many men, in their teaching and in their lectures, can do an admirable and necessary job of keeping alive their strain of the intellectual tradition, and of imparting the genuine joys, and excitement to be gained from first-hand acquaintance with the major texts of civilization.

The bearing of the three citations which began this paper may now be clearer. Jim Dixon has drifted into a subject for research which his better judgment finally tells him is ridiculous. Responsive to what is worst in the mindless rituals of academic life, he has undertaken a busy-work project humanly useless to him. Worse than that, since one becomes what he persistently chooses, a sequence of such choices would negate Jim as a human being and make of him a juiceless fool like the pedantic Professor Welch.

On the other hand, the possibility for authentic communication is opened by Johannes Climacus' decision to make things harder by choosing to tell the existential truth about man's ambiguous condition, his capacity for self-transcendence, and his being subject to a death which hangs over him every instant. Authentic communication between persons is possible only as the consequence of relentless honesty, when all the socially-settled roles and psychologically-protective masks are dropped so that the mystery of direct confrontation can occur. There are dangers to be risked in breaking the barriers that keep us from insight and sympathy, for as at least one existentialist has indicated, in removing the mask of a ghost or a goblin we do not find a child asking for candy on Halloween but something even more horrible than the mask itself.

Professor Auer's suggestion that one justifiable motive for picking a topic is that investigating it may result in publication must be rejected. To publish for the sake of publishing, with its consequence of getting "a name in the field" and strengthening one's academic respectability, is to act in bad faith.

For an existentialist, one never chooses subjects: he chooses himself and what he is to be. Speech, concerned with our most crucially human act, has special obligations to act in good faith, to repudiate the manipulative designs of communications engineers, and to assert and demonstrate in all its studies the truth in Karl Jaspers' beliefs that "I am only in conjunction with another," and that authentic communication between persons results from "a loving contest in which each surrenders his weapons to the other." The existentialist view, if taken seriously, would seem to have these consequences: (1) The problems one chooses to study and the way in which they are studied are more radically important than has usually been recognized or acknowledged. (2) Preparation for significant studies in speech should be based on an understanding of the fundamental differences between qualitative humanistic knowledge and quantitative scientific knowledge. (3) Frequently, it will be much better—and not as a result of weakness or evasion—not to undertake publication-directed research. But any paper, thesis, dissertation, article, or book—published or unpublished—should give, in Warren and Wellek's words, "a real sample of its author's intellectual quality . . . Mere industry and endurance are not intellectual virtues." Or moral ones, either, it should be added.

Earlier I remarked that, in public address, no study of a speaker is complete without responsible ethical evaluation. Let me here suggest what existentialism would say about some of the sillinesses in the oral interpretation of poetry—the embarrassing gestures, the pregnant pauses that never deliver anything, the notoriously inept changes in pitch and pace. Though often such weaknesses reveal innate deficiencies in intelligence and sensitivity, the trouble frequently results from unconscious or willing acceptance of the scientific divorce between thought and feeling. In such dichotomies, poetry is parcelled out to feeling, and the interpreter believes he must give his audience emotional fireworks. But seen properly, a successful poem is a product of the author's uniquely personal vision, and gives knowledge of a new reality created (or perhaps discovered) by the poet's aesthetic resolution of fact, judgment, emotion, and sensation into something different in character from any one of them. If a poem is total, and absolute, and committed in this way, then a proper approach to it will understand that the poet's ordering of the words will in itself carry the burden of his statement. In oral reading, elocutionary tricks are not only not necessary, but positively distorting. Studies in oral interpretation will be most successful when they are based on a knowledge of what the object is with which the interpreter works.

This paper has been largely negative in trying to say what seems to be wrong. And though any impact it may have had would be greater if stronger, established scholars had said these things, perhaps it will have the purgative effect necessary as our official memos to the world and to ourselves that all is well, and that all we need is more of the same old thing, are betrayed by the uneasy feeling in many teachers that in many ways for many years we have been mining fool's gold.

The Wondering
and Wandering Jew
in Malamud's Fiction

Delivered at the Third Annual
Scholars in Residence Program
Congregation Solel, Highland Park, Illinois,
March 11-13, 1977

The characters and plots of Malamud's fiction explore implicitly and, at times, explicitly what is Jewishness. Beyond the practices of religious law and worship place, Jews suffer and sacrifice in their need to serve humanity and to worship God. Malamud does not, finally, resolve the problem of whether there is any metaphysical and psychological essence that is Jewishness," in its evolving presence through history "beyond articulation in discursive words."

I give this presentation with the special enabling (or crippling) circumstance that I myself am a Jew, although from many accounts (including sometimes my own) I am a Jew manqué; that is, one who is in some sense defective, or at least has not achieved the quality expected of him. You will see that a bristling host of difficult questions are implicit in that statement: among them, and basic to them all, is the question, What is a Jew? And beyond that, what special problems, if any, arise when Jewish materials are used in literature, particularly when a Jewish reader reads? Does being Jewish, in whatever sense the word is defined, qualify or disqualify the reader from making sound literary judgments? Or is the whole consideration irrelevant?

Before suggesting how these questions relate to my defining perspective and concern—namely, the wondering and wandering Jew in

Malamud's fiction—let me first make a few overall observations. If you are interested in one of the most lyric, cleanest literary styles of our time, you should read Malamud. If you are interested in seeing how the comic and tragic, sometimes even the sublime and the ridiculous, can unite in the same episode, you should read him. If you are interested, in Alfred Kazin's words, "in returning to life . . . in its beautiful and inexpressible materiality—life as the gift it actually is rather than the 'material' that we try to remake," you should read him. If you have a taste for the unique way in which the paradoxical and enigmatic can combine with the most pellucidly elemental vision, you should read Malamud.

And in a few weeks you can read the bulk of what he has written. Nearing 63, Malamud has published nine relatively short books— three collections of short stories, five novels, and one work (*Pictures of Fidelman*) that is really a collection of stories, but in which a unifying main character appears in each tale.

As I proceed, you will recognize that in my extracting remarks about the books I will be doing some violence on what finally makes Malamud worth reading, since full literary import is not only, or even primarily, a matter of "idea" or "message," but depends, rather, on a dramatic juxtaposition of allusive scene, a skillful use of metaphor, compelling depiction of character, and the necessary grace of an all-suffusing stylistic rhythm. With that caveat, I now turn directly to these most engaging works.

Of *The Natural* (1952), Malamud's earliest book and one of his few works without specifically religious or ethnic materials, I will say only that with the passionate excitement that baseball can engender as his nominal subject, Malamud elevates to mythological significance such historic facts as Shoeless Joe Jackson's treachery in the 1919 World Series, Babe Ruth's mighty gastronomic feats, the incredible pennant surges of the 1914 Boston Braves and the 1951 New York Giants, and the shooting of the Philadelphia Phillies' first-baseman, Eddie Waitkus, by a deranged female fan some thirty years ago. But the real themes of the book are the hysteria of insensate competition, the warped sexuality behind much hero worship, the vicious moles in nature revealed and encouraged by spectator passivity, the beauty of innocence and the ugliness of its corruption. Woven throughout is an ingenuous admiration for the natural skill of Roy Hobbs, the simple and single-minded hero, who sets record after record until he is betrayed by his own limitations and the predatory world of organized sport. *The Natural* is a bizarrely brilliant achievement with a hauntingly alien overtone that works in more subdued shadings in several of the stories in *The Magic Barrel*.

With the exception of *The Natural* and some of the short stories, all of Malamud's fiction published in book form has Jews as central characters, and frequently makes adroit use of the unmistakable idiom of the Jewish immigrant, with its ellipses, inversions of phrase, humorous grammatical twists, occasional slanginess, and pervasive emotionalism of outrage, indignity, or imploring entreaty. Thus, in the story "The Mourners," old Kessler, the former egg candler, is being dispossessed, and says bitterly to his Jewish landlord: "'What did I do to you?' he bitterly wept, 'Who throws out of his house a man that he lived there ten years and pays every month on time his rent? What did I do, tell me? Who hurts a man without a reason? Are you a Hitler or a Jew?' He was hitting his chest with his fist." Or listen to the tailor Manischevitz, from the story "Angel Levine." Manischevitz, a modern-day Job in his heaped-up sufferings, prays: "'My dear God, sweetheart, did I deserve that this should happen to me?' Then recognizing the worthlessness of it, he put aside the complaint and prayed humbly for assistance: 'Give Fanny back her health, and to me for myself that I shouldn't feel pain in every step. Help now or tomorrow is too late. This I don't have to tell you.' And Manischevitz wept." Or in the fantasy "Take Pity," Rosen is telling Davidov, a census-taker in heaven, how Axel Kalish, an impoverished refugee, father of two little girls, Fega and Surale, has dropped dead:

> "How did he die?'" Davidov spoke impatiently. "Say in one word."
> "From what he died?—he died, that's all."
> "Answer, please this question.."
> "Broke in him something. That's how."
> "Broke what?"
> "Broke what breaks. He was talking to me how bitter was his life, and he touched me on my sleeve to say something else,

but the next minute his face got small and he fell down dead, the wife screaming, the little girls crying that it made in my heart pain. I am myself a sick man and when I saw him lying on the floor, I said to myself, 'Rosen, say goodbye, this guy is finished.' So I said it."

Your smiles reveal that you have recognized the inevitable inflection of your parents or grandparents, or maybe of yourselves, and have just heard reaffirmed the traditional notions that a Jew should not hurt a Jew, that a Jew is one who suffers, that God has a strange way of treating his chosen ones.

But only rarely in his fiction does Malamud raise directly the problem of what a Jew is. In the novel, *The Assistant*, published twenty years ago, Morris Bober, one of Malamud's many strugglingly unsuccessful shopkeepers, is questioned by Frank Alpine, the Italian who enters the story by robbing Morris and leaves it by being circumcised as part of becoming a Jew.

"Say Morris, suppose somebody asked you what do the Jews believe in, what would you tell them?"

The grocer stopped peeling, unable at once to reply. "What I like to know is what is a Jew anyway?'"

Because he was ashamed of his meager education Morris was never comfortable with such questions, yet he felt he must answer.

"My father used to say to be a Jew all you need is a good heart."

"What do you say?"

"The important thing is the Torah. That is the Law—a Jew must believe in the Law."

"Let me ask you this," Frank went on. "Do you consider yourself a real Jew?"

Morris was startled, "What do you mean if I am a real Jew?"

"Don't get sore about this," Frank said, "But I can give you an argument that you aren't. First thing, you don't go to the synagogue—not that I have ever seen. You don't keep your kitchen kosher and you don't eat kosher. You don't even wear one of those little black hats like this tailor I knew in South Chicago. He prayed three times a day. I even hear the Mrs. say you kept the store open on Jewish holidays, it makes no difference if she yells her head off."

"Sometimes," Morris answered, flushing, "to have to eat, you must keep open on holidays. On Yom Kippur I don't keep open. But I don't worry about kosher, which is to me old-fashioned. What I worry is to follow the Jewish law."

"But all those things are the Law, aren't they? And don't the Law say you can't eat any pig, but I have seen you taste ham."

"This is not important to me if I taste pig or if I don't. To some Jews is this important but not to me. Nobody will tell me that I am not Jewish because I put in my mouth once in a while, when my tongue is dry, a piece ham. But they will tell me, and I will believe them, if I forget the Law. This means to do what is right, to be honest, to be good. This means to other people. Our life is hard enough. Why should we hurt somebody else? For everybody should be the best, not only for you or me. We ain't animals. This is why we need the Law. This is what a Jew believes."

"I think other religions have these ideas too," Frank said. "But tell me why is it that the Jews suffer so damn much, Morris? It seems to me that they like to suffer, don't they?"

"Do you like to suffer? They suffer because they are Jews."

"That's what I mean, they suffer more than they have to."

"If you live, you suffer. Some people suffer more, but not because they want. But I think if a Jew don't suffer for the Law, he will suffer for nothing."

"What do you suffer for, Morris?" Frank said.

"I suffer for you," Morris said calmly. (It develops that Morris knows that Frank is the one who had robbed him.) A bit later, Morris ends by saying, "If a Jew forgets the Law . . . he is not a good Jew, and not a good man."

In similar vein, the poet and critic, Karl Shapiro, in a provocative essay, "The Jewish Writer in America," argues that Saul Bellow's *The*

Adventures of Augie March "is saturated with Jewish witticisms and sentiments" but that what "is really Jewish in Bellow lies much deeper: it is the poetry of the Jew that makes his hero what he is, in Chicago, in Mexico, wherever Augie happens to be. . . . This is Jewishness far beyond culture, social problems, history, and the rest. It is even beyond religion." Yet, for Shapiro, true Jewishness must be God-centered, though he believes that being God-centered need not have connection with ritual or ritualistic piety. Shapiro paraphrases the Jewish existentialist thinker, Martin Buber: "The true hallowing of man is the hallowing of the human in him. . . . Man . . . cannot approach the divine by reaching beyond the human; but he can approach Him through becoming human."

You know the wealth of response such statements can elicit from the wide spectrum of modern Jewry, or how similar consideration can upset traditionalists of any religious persuasion. The extremely orthodox will look upon any departure from ancient practices as something almost as heinous as marrying outside the faith; the conservative will point to his blending of the old and the new as an intelligent adaptation of eternal truths to the evolving conditions of modern life; and the reform Jew who goes to the temple for any other reason than social pressure or unreflecting conformity will often doubt that there are any eternal truths, and will accept his not-too-carefully defined Jewishness as a given fact of existence. How much creed and what kind is necessary in order to be Jewish? How much ritual? What is the proper relationship of creed to ritual? Is ritual a pleasant accessory to dogma, or its inescapable poetry, necessary for disposing our hearts to love and reverence? Is Jewishness, like perhaps nearly everything else, a matter of labeling and historical accident someday to disappear completely? Or is there any metaphysical and psychological essence that is distinctively Jewish?

Malamud's fiction does not resolve these problems, but it implicitly raises them. In fact, Malamud as writer perhaps realizes the dangers he faces, and relatively early in his career at times became so careful about letting his Jewish concern be obtrusive that in the novel, *A New Life*, published in 1961, the hero, Seymour Levin, clearly Jewish, is never referred to as such, and in every external way leads a completely non-Jewish life. Yet, as I shall show later, the question of what it is to be a Jew is a powerful undercurrent in that novel, shaping almost every episode.

A central problem of the author who uses members of minority groups as his main characters is to escape the limits of simple local color and regional writing, to transcend the temporal which may have some flavorful curiosity value but can never confer true stature to a writer. As Shapiro puts it, a "merely Judaistic literature is only a kind of 'regional' literature, even though this 'region' takes in most of the world and all of history. In such literature the Jew may be good or bad, Shylock or The Wandering Jew or Leopold Bloom, but he is simply a man of memory, an anachronism. He is not the Jew who 'lives life,' as Martin Buber puts it. He is the Jew of the past, the Jew of the Wailing Wall."

Though Shapiro minimizes the importance of the past, failing to recognize its crucial role in forming the psyche of the modern Jew, he rightly sees that unless the Jew in literature is portrayed as one who "lives life," whose historic commitment to the Law is expressed in a variety of poetic guises, then there will be not literature, but only exclusivist anecdotalism, ethnic curiosa, and sentimental reminiscence. Apart from its polished craftsmanship, Malamud's fiction has great worth because his Jews do "live life," having or seeking an elemental joy, and shedding tears that grieve on universal bones. This is not to say that Malamud makes individual Jews better than they often are—in his own words, there are *goniffs*, *schnorrers*, *schnooks*, *schmos* and *schlmiels*; there are the self-pitying, the self-righteous; and perhaps reflecting a slight weakness in Malamud himself, characters who sometimes give into a clownish self-deprecation that is not always appropriate.

There are potential assimilationists in irresponsible flight from the burdens of Jewishness; there are wheedlers who use the claim of Jewish blood-kinship to become parasites; there are the belligerent and cocksure, the snivelling and writhing, the hen-pecked and softly obsequious. But, more positively, there are the industrious, the toilers, those who respect learning, the patient sufferers of reversal, the courteous, those who strive to breathe a cleaner air, to live a new life, to escape all that is humanly degrading in any ghetto-like restriction. There are those whose lack of formal learning cannot obscure the lambent wisdom gained from oppression and the quintessential humanity of the enduring Jewish emphasis on a sane ethics.

As commentator, I have just done some generalizing, which Malamud as creative writer does not do. The characters and episodes in his works which allow these generalized conclusions are presented concretely and dramatically, though often with an intriguing incompleteness that reflects a typical Jewish strength of not claiming to know more than can be known. In the major part of my presentation, I want mainly to make some summaries and glosses that will help clarify what I have said so far, and will, I hope, whet your desire to read or reread.

The novel, *The Assistant*, is Malamud's most straightforward and transparent work. Morris Bober, whom we have heard speak earlier, labors in his little grocery store against the competition of modern supermarkets, against his recurring grief over the memory of his dead son, against his feeling of guilt and helplessness that his daughter, Helen, now 23, has had to give up her education to get a job to help her parents. All the materials for a tenth-rate soap opera are here, but Malamud's genius for transmuting base metal into shining gold makes *The Assistant* a modern parable that reaffirms the intrinsic and unarguable value of simple goodness. Frank Alpine, the drifter, who robs Morris, then becomes his assistant, then robs him again, then attempts a near-rape of his daughter, is gradually, painfully, and subtly changed, and finally reborn, by the example of Morris's un¬wavering integrity. After Morris dies, Frank is circumcised in process of becoming a Jew, with the pain in his flesh a symbol of the pain that had been in his spirit as he had learned the meaning of suffering.

The short stories in *The Magic Barrel* (1958) are more oblique. There are many silences of vast implication, silences which give the haunting, inconclusive quality I have spoken of earlier. In "The First Seven Years," the shortsightedness of the Jewish father who wishes his daughter to make a good match is amusingly portrayed. Feld, the shoemaker, wants his daughter, Miriam, to go out with Max, a student, one who will be a professional man (though Feld finds, to his temporary disappointment, a C.P.A. rather than a doctor or lawyer). Feld does not see at first that the materialistic Max is completely wrong for his sensitive daughter, who is quietly loved by Feld's assistant for five years, Sobel, an immigrant greenhorn, but a reader of books, dreamy and introspective. Finally, the father asks Sobel to wait two years before asking for Miriam's hand: will there then be seven years of plenty after the seven years of famine?

In "The Mourners," two old Jews, Kessler and Gruber, to whom we have referred before (Are you a Hitler or a Jew?), in the stark confrontation of the attempted dispossession of Kessler from Gruber's apartment house, suddenly recover from the barrenness of their sour and empty lives, and in a tenderly grotesque tableau ı rap sheets about themselves and sink to the floor of Kessler's filthy apartment as mourners in a weird *kaddish*, a prayer for the dead strains in their own dead lives and the lives of those whom they have failed.

"The Girl of My Dreams" presents Mitka, the aspiring but enormously untalented writer, who engages in a correspondence with a girl, so he thinks, with the romantic name Madeline Thorn. He arranges to meet her and finds she is a somewhat lumpish older woman named Olga—one more disappointment. Olga and Mitka sit down to a feast of salmon and black bread; and when Mitka returns to his rooming house, in a what-the-hell mood he finally succumbs to the blandishments of his landlady, Mrs. Lutz, a kind of lecherous Molly Goldberg. The story is funny and sad—the special Jewish desire to excel cut down to size when aspiration foolishly runs ahead of ability. But Malamud, here as so often, poignantly suggests that existence may be supportable only when one lives it in the dream of a better, a new life.

"Angel Levine," a tantalizing fantasy, has Manischevitz's prayer, cited earlier, answered in the form of an unlikely Harlem Negro, a black Jewish angel, named Levine. Manischevitz is properly incredulous, but after his wife, Fanny, is on her deathbed and his own ailments are unbearable, he goes to search out Levine. The angel has lost his dignified bearing and presumably his power, until Manischevitz says that he believes, whereupon Levine sets all ills aright. The story ends with Manischevitz saying to his wife: "A wonderful thing, Fanny. . . . Believe me, there are Jews everywhere." Make of *that* one what you will. Is it about the power of faith? Is it that rare thing, a call for Jewish catholicity: if Marilyn Monroe and Elizabeth Taylor and Sammy Davis can *really* be Jews, why not Angel Levine?

Rosen, the ex-coffee salesman and central figure in the story "Take Pity," whose account of Alex Kalish's death we have already heard, tries to assist Alex's widow, Eva, mother of little Fega and Surale. But his irresistible desire to help is matched by her unmovable intention not to be helped. Malamud suggests a rock-ribbed monomania on both sides, but Rosen, at least, is heroic: "'Here,' I said to myself, 'is a very strange thing—a person that you can never give her anything.—*But I will give*.'" And Rosen finally gave all by signing over his possessions to Eva, then committing suicide. As Rosen finishes talking in the murky heaven where Davidov is taking account, Eva appears outside his window—apparently dead too, but now holding out her arms supplicatingly toward him.

> Infuriated, the ex-salesman shook his fist. "Whore, bastard, bitch," he shouted at her. "Go 'way from here. Go home to your children."

Is the story about Jewish generosity, stubbornness, futility? When does perseverance (perhaps even perseverance in surviving as a people) become a self-destructive obstinacy?

In "The Last Mohican," Arthur Fidelman, the critic and failed painter, arrives in Rome and almost at once is accosted by what surely must be one of the biggest pests in all literature, one Shimon Susskind, who presumes on their shared Jewishness to hound Fidelman to near-despair. Susskind, that unlikely thing, a Jewish refugee from Israel, hucksters and pan-handles his way through Italy, and with bumptious self-assurance marks out Fidelman as his special victim. Midway in the story, Fidelman cries: ". . . why pick on me? Am I responsible for you then, Susskind?"

> "Who else?" Susskind loudly replied.
>
> "Lower your voice, please, people are sleeping around here," said Fidelman, beginning to perspire. "Why should I be?"
>
> "You know what responsibility means?"
>
> "I think so."
>
> "Then you are responsible. Because you are a man. Because you are a Jew aren't you?"

"Yes, goddamn it, but I'm not the only one in the whole wide world. Without prejudice, I refuse the obligation. I am a single individual and can't take on every body's personal burden. I have the weight of my own to contend with."

But at the end, his manuscript stolen by Susskind, Fidelman is yet ready to give Susskind the suit he has asked for from their first meeting. In a savagely comic conclusion, Fidelman is chasing Susskind as the "ghetto Jews, framed in amazement in their medieval windows, stared at the wild pursuit . . . 'Susskind, come back. . . . The suit is yours. All is forgiven.'" The questions the story dramatizes certainly include: Are all Jews brothers? and, if so, is each Jew his brother's keeper?

In "The Loan," two old friends, Kabotsky the baker, and Lieb the former furcutter, who had parted 15 years before because of a disagreement over money, come together in Lieb's bakery, where Kabotsky seeks a loan to buy a gravestone for his five-years-dead wife. But Lieb has a wife, Bessie, who seizes upon Kabotsky's grief as occasion for venting her own. All three, in their various ways, are soon aware that the estrangements of circumstance, time, and one's peculiar suffering shut out the help that one would give. At the end, "Kabotsky and the baker embraced and sighed over their lost youth. They pressed mouths together and parted forever." The story is beautifully done; it is replete with rich symbols: charred loaves recalling the charred bodies of Hitler's incinerators; Lieb's bread being sought only after he had wept tears into the dough after thirty penniless years. And throughout, there is the special charm of Malamud's saving humor.

The title story, "The Magic Barrel," is perhaps the best of the group. Leo Finkel, rabbinical student, hoping to get a wife before he gets his first pulpit, enlists the aid of Pinye Salzman, *shotchun*, marriage broker. Pinye is a smelly modern-day cupid, with a greasy portfolio in which he carries not only smoked fish but his packet of vitae sheets and photos of harried spinsters, all described by Pinye in the glowing terms of a pitchman who half believes what he says. Leo's delicacy at what has become of what was once the honored Jewish tradition of the marriage-broker leads him to some agonizing introspection, in which he thinks that he has come to God not because he loved Him so much but rather because he loved Him so little. Finally, he sees by accident—or is it?—a girl's photo which goes straight to his heart. Salzman, aghast, says this is no girl for a rabbi; it is his own daughter whose shame at her poverty has driven her to the streets. But Leo will not be denied. The story ends with Leo meeting Stella at a street corner—the painted woman under the lamp luring the innocent, or is Stella the desperately innocent waiting to be loved? Around the corner, Salzman is saying prayers for the dead. Is Salzman charlatan or saint? Is Malamud saying, with Buber, that in life as Jewish mysticism "understands and proclaims it, there is no essential distinction between sacred and profane spaces, between sacred and profane times, between sacred and profane actions, between sacred and profane conversations"?

The final story in *The Magic Barrel* mirroring the Jewish predicament, and one that will serve as a bridge to a consideration of the novel, *A New Life*, is "The Lady of the Lake." The title refers to the romantic heroine of Sir Walter Scott's famous poem, but the lady of this story, after innocently masquerading for a time as an Italian noblewoman, Isabella del Dongo, turns out to be a Jewish refugee, daughter of the caretaker on an Italian estate. She wishes to marry an American, Henry Levin, who in Europe calls himself Henry F. Freeman, and even thinks of changing his name from Levin to LeVin. At their first meeting, when Levin thinks the girl is Italian, she asks him point-blank if he is Jewish. He denies it, but is curious as to why she asks. He reflects that she would not want to marry a Jew, but concludes that, if he brought her to the States, after a time she would see that "it was no crime to be Jewish; that a man's past was, it could safely be said, expendable." Besides, he thinks, what had being Jewish "brought him but headaches, inferiorities, unhappy memories?" He is further baffled when, once on an outing, Isabella points to the Alps, and says to Levin: "Don't those peaks—those seven—look like a Menorah?" And at the end, she asks him once more if he is Jewish. He continues to deny it. She unbuttons her bodice and reveals her breasts: "to his horror he discerned tattooed on the soft and tender flesh a bluish line of distorted numbers," the work of the Nazis at Buchenwald. She tells Levin, "I can't marry you. We are Jews. My past is meaningful to me. I treasure what I suffer for."

Who is right, Levin or Isabella? Is a Jew's past expendable? If it were, could Levin in literal fact become Freeman? The question seemed an overriding concern with Malamud in his novel, *A New Life*, published in 1961. The book had a mixed reception, some thinking that it was a falling off from his earlier writing, another weary tale of adultery on the college campus. And some could see no reason why its hero is Jewish, arguing that he might just as well have been the son of a prosperous Protestant insurance salesman from Evanston. On the contrary, I find the book more interesting than any of the work up to that time. It is rich in paradoxes and ironies; and the near-burlesque, parody, and farce of much of its style and content prevents the genuine sadness of its hero, another Levin, this one Seymour, from becoming sentimental. Most of the Jewish themes of Malamud's other work are present, but here veiled in a realistic allegory of many reflecting mirrors.

The very title itself, *A New Life*, is an ironic echo of Dante's *La Vita Nuova*, in which that great poet told how his life was utterly changed by his meeting with Beatrice. Levin, an oldish instructor at a Western college, meets not Beatrice, but Pauline Gilley, the chronically malcontent wife of his composition chairman, the smugly complacent Gerald Gilley. And as Dante's mastering concern was to achieve his salvation, so Seymour Levin is in flight from his embittered and benighted past, in search of, in his words, "order, value, accomplishment, love." He is in flight from his *goniff* father, and his mother, who had killed herself. He is in flight from his own past drunkenness, from the teeming East. Is he in flight from his Jewishness? Can this Jew escape his identity? Will he always be an alien, an outsider, alluded to, as here, not directly as Jew, but as city-boy, as intellectual, as wearer of a beard, as troublemaker? Will he overcome his own strange culturally inherited mixture of idealism and ineptitude? Can he respond to the beneficent restorative power of the cyclic changes in nature after life-long deprivation? How will he define his role as teacher and scholar, particularly in an atmosphere actually hostile to real thinking and feeling? Cut off by choice and by circumstance from dead or dying roots, what new ones can he sink?

Levin is a blend of J. Alfred Prufrock, Don Quixote, Walter Mitty, and the innocent bystander; but he is also amazingly clear-sighted about the abuse of authority, the sterility of much in modern education, and though not in any obvious sense, the claims of fidelity. The index to his human condition, and perhaps to his Jewish predicament, is found in the allusively compressed opening sentences of the novel. "S. Levin, formerly a drunkard, after a long and tiring transcontinental journey, got off the train at Marathon, Cascadia, toward evening of the last Sunday in August, 1950. Bearded, fatigued, lonely, Levin set down a valise and suitcase and looked around in a strange land for welcome." Later that evening at the Gilleys, Levin reveals his "...hopes that a new place will inspire change—in one's life," and further, that in the past he had cheated himself and killed his choices.

Levin keeps a book of insights, insights which show that he is aware that his past may well be his fate: "The new life hangs on an old soul"; "I am one who creates his own peril"; "The danger of the times is the betrayal of man." He attempts to forge significant relationships, but for a time they take only the form of abortive sexual interludes with a waitress, a painfully unmarried female colleague, and one of his girl students, who has the good Nordic name of Nadalee Hammerstad. Cascadia (really Oregon, where Malamud taught for many years at Oregon State) is a physical paradise, though the rainy season often causes an inferno-like drooping of spirits. Paradise can be false-paradise too, as Levin discovers after a purgatorial ascent over the Coast Range mountains to keep an assignation with Nadalee in a deserted motel by the Pacific. A short time later, Levin and Nadalee are engaged in a hassle over grades, in which Levin has to consider the fine moral point of whether he owes anything as teacher to a girl student by whom he has been, not unwillingly, seduced. Later he has to face a somewhat similar decision about Pauline Gilley, a woman whom he for a time genuinely if ambivalently loves, but who is, after all, the wife of the man who gave him a job. Yet it develops that Levin had been hired because Gilley had let his wife pick out an instructor from a huge stack of applications. She had picked him because, as she says, "Your picture reminded me of a Jewish boy I knew in college who was very kind to me during a trying time in my life." It is the only time the word "Jew" or "Jewish" is used in the novel. And Levin's response is revealing: "So I was chosen," Levin said.

So this Jew has been chosen, but by whom and for what? And how chosen, but by an absurd incident in which he has moved a neurotic yet valorous woman in an impressionable moment? Trapped more than liberated, Levin, discovered in his adultery with Pauline, is dismissed from his job and drives off in his old Hudson, tragically yet comically, with the now pregnant-by-him Pauline and her two adopted children. What has the new life brought? What can it bring? Or is it that for the Jew cut off from his past there can be no defined new life but only the unending and unpromising process of seeking fresh identity?

Several of the eleven stories in the 1963 collection of tales, *Idiots First*, look back to Malamud's earlier work or forward to books which were to come later. For example, the story "A Choice of Profession" appears to be a study for *A New Life*, and "The Cost of Living" a kind of trial version of what later became *The Assistant*. Two stories featuring Arthur Fidelman, who was first met in "The Last Mohican" in *The Magic Barrel*, appear with that story later in Malamud's book published in 1969 entitled *Pictures of Fidelman*.

Let me comment briefly on three of the stories in *Idiots First* which represent Malamud's continuing concern with Jewish alienation and the precarious position of the Jew in the modern world. In the story "Black Is My Favorite Color," much of whose theme will receive powerful statement in 1971 in the novel *The Tenants*, Malamud begins to explore the relationships between Jews and blacks. Nat Lime, a forty-four year old bachelor who lives in a section of New York, has an affair with a black women, Ornita, whose male friends don't understand and obviously don't approve of this kind of relationship. One day one of them slugs Nat, who asks, "Why did you do it? What did I do to you?" The black answers, "Because you a Jew bastard. Take your Jew movies and your Jew candy and shove them up your Jew ass." That's the kind of treatment Nat gets throughout the story. He remembers his mother who said, "If you ever forget you are a Jew, a goy will remind you." Nat tries hard to be reasonable and reachable, but he speculates philosophically at the end: "That's how it is. I give my heart and they kick me in my teeth."

In the delightful fantasy entitled "The Jewbird," a bird one day flies into the window of Harry Cohen's apartment. As he comes in the bird says, "Gevalt, a pogrom." Harry's wife Edie says, "It's a talking bird." And their son Maurie says, "In Jewish." Cohen mutters, "Wise guy! If you can talk say what's your business, what do you want here?" "If you can't spare a lamb chop," said the bird, "I'll settle for a piece

of herring with a crust of bread. You can't live on your nerve forever."
"This ain't a restaurant," Cohen replied. "All I'm asking is what brings
you to this address." "The window was open," the bird sighed, adding
after a moment: "I'm running; I'm flying, but I'm also running." "From
whom," asked Edie with interest. "Anti-Semites." "Anti-Semites?"
they all said. "That's from who." "What kind of Anti-Semites bother
a bird?" Edie asked. "Any kind" said the bird, "also including eagles,
vultures and hawks and once in a while some crows will take your eyes
out." "But aren't you a crow?" "Me? I'm a Jewbird." Cohen laughed
heartily. "What do you mean by that? The bird began dovening. He
prayed without book or talith but with passion." When throughout
the next several days the bird keep asking for more and more Harry
becomes increasingly irritated and finally scats the bird away, because
Harry says, "you're an A-number-1 trouble maker, you got to get out of
here." After the bird (called Schwartz by the way) has gone they find it
dead in a field. The son cries, "Who did it to you Mr. Schwartz?" His
mother Edie said later, "Anti-Semites did it."

What does Malamud suggest? That the whole natural order is hostile to the stranger, the outsider, the Jew—whether in human form or
in bird form? Is the Jew an enemy to himself? Later Malamud is to
write about a Jew in the form of a horse, who struggles to get out of
the particular bind that he's in.

A somber and moving story is the one entitled "The German Refugee," which looks forward in some respects to the novel *The Fixer*,
which was to be published three years later in 1966. In this story, Oskar
Gassner, who has fled from the emerging Hitler regime in Germany,
is an educated man, a professor. He has come to the East Coast where
he is preparing lectures on Whitman and other writers, scheduled to
be given the following fall. But his confidence has been so shattered
by the experience he has had in Germany during those terrible years
which were to get worse that, with her accord, he has left his gentile
wife and come to America. He struggles with his German tongue, not
because he's incapable of learning English but because his sensibilities
have been so dampened and demeaned by what he has seen that he
tells the young American student Martin Goldberg, who is tutoring
him, "Confidenze I have not. For thiz and alzo whatever elze I have
lozt I thank the Nazis."

But under the care of Martin he does master English sufficiently and prepares his lectures on the spirit of freedom. Shortly after September 1939 when Hitler has marched on Poland, there is an emergency call to Gassner's apartment. The police find that he has killed himself. They discover that a letter has been written from his wife who had converted to Judaism. Gassner had learned that one night the brown shirts appeared. They had taken his wife and other Jews out of the apartment house and transported them in lorries to a small border town in conquered Poland. "There it was rumored she was shot in the head and toppled into an open tank ditch with the naked Jewish men, their wives and children, some Polish soldiers, and a handful of Gypsies." Here is the remembrance of the Holocaust, which continued to haunt so many aspects of Malamud's fiction, whatever the setting of these gross indignities. Gassner is different from many of Malamud's émigrés and refugees, most of whom as we have seen and will see are shopkeepers, tailors, grocers, handymen. This is a cultivated man, but of course to the scourge of Anti-Semitism all Jews are alike.

The sixth of Malamud's nine published books appeared in 1966. *The Fixer* may be the best of the nine, but fortunately one doesn't have to make choices; we have all of them. This wondrously moving book has for its first epigraph a line from the poet Yeats, "Irrational streams of blood are staining earth." Those of you who know it will recall that it is a tale of a simple Russian Jewish handyman's unmerited sufferings, recounted in a sustained unfolding of all the conceivable implications of Yeats's line, "Irrational streams of blood are staining earth."

Yakov Bok is arrested on a trumped up charge that he has killed a Christian boy in an act of ritual murder. Tormented by the knowledge of his own innocence and by every kind of personal humiliation, he withers in prison for more than two years before he is brought to a trial which will undoubtedly find him guilty. His only crime is that he is a Jew, for which (as Malamud implies throughout his work) you might substitute any era's particular outsider. But Bok serves at this time and at this place as the marked out victim of the monstrous irrationalities that have riven heaven and earth throughout man's tragic history. By any external estimate he is one more figure in the long gallery of Malamud's doomed aspirants to a new life, a life free from the ghettos of ignorance, poverty, failure, and abuse. But by every relevant consideration of the spirit he is a towering example of why, even in the face of so much contrary evidence, it is yet possible to have undimmed hope for man. His wanderings have taken him only from a little shtetl to Kiev, where he does a kind act for a Russian member of the violently anti-Jewish dreaded Black Hundreds. Nonetheless he is arrested. He contemplates suicide and rejects it, hoping for an ultimate justice that perhaps can be no more than one's own fully believed self-vindication. He is promised release if he will implicate others, but he will not betray his fellow Jews even though he is a free thinker who tries poignantly to read his gritty experience in the light of the Spinozist idealism Malamud juxtaposes with loving irony to the messiness of the existing world.

For all its portrayal of horrible events *The Fixer* is not a grim book. As always in Malamud there is a saving light touch which shows most characteristically in an unrivaled instinct for humorous self-deprecation—a kind of secular equivalent to religious humility. Yakov says:

> "I incline toward the philosophical, although I don't know much about anything."
> "I fix what's broken, except in the heart."
> "Who invented my life?"
> "If I'm going to be ashamed of anyone it might as well be myself."
> "I am a fixer but all my life I have broken more than I fix."

By making no extraordinary claims for man Malamud builds a case for man better than he knows—except that he does know. The continuing paradox of his work up to the time of the publishing of *The Fixer*—and since for that matter—is that he is able to invest his leading personages with his own highly aware sensitivities, at the same time keeping them elementally simple in ways that bespeak the sacramental qualities in human life. Thus Yakov Bok, his father-in-law Schmul, his wife Raisl, and the magistrate Bibikov are among those tendered with taut directness of style and deftly precise character sketching which makes them rich symbols of what Malamud, as we have seen earlier in *A New Life*, has called man's need for value, order, accomplishment, love.

In the intense drama of this book what might have been empty preachments become agonizing particularistic necessities. "Keep in mind that if your life is without value so is mine." "What suffering has taught me is the uselessness of suffering." "If I have any philosophy it's that life could be better than it is." "We all have to be reasonable or what's bad gets worse." "Live and let live if you don't mind me saying so. It's a short life when you think of it." *The Fixer* is a book which itself weeps for the tears of things. It sees redemption not in suffering but in *rochmones*—mercy. It is a searing exposure and indictment of the moral schizophrenia that can make Eichmanns out of banal men. It reminds us that the purpose of freedom is to create it for others, that through vision of what might be and through "remembrance of green things growing on earth" the heart can ache beyond belief.

. . .

What is a modern thinker, and particularly a twentieth century American Jew, to make of the questions raised by Malamud's fiction, how to interpret the old saw that God chose the Jews because the Jews chose God? Remembering Pauline Gilley in *A New Life*, who had chosen Levin almost at random from a group of photographs, we might ask if history itself has not been a kind of Pauline Gilley, absurdly yet triumphantly marking out this nation, this race, this religion, this cultural community, this mystical brotherhood, this invented scapegoat, this whetstone on which much of mankind has been forced to sharpen its moral conscience—all the things the Jews at one time or another have been held to be or have held themselves to be. Is there something uniquely worth preserving in Jewishness? Or is being parochial in any sense a necessity or a luxury that human kind no longer needs or can no longer afford? Is *any* parochial identity, no matter how comprehensive, relevant to the demands of an increasingly secular and dangerous world? If there is to be a truly universal brotherhood, will it come at the cost of a pallid sameness we can neither foresee, nor would accept if we did? Is it possible that each religious, racial, national, or cultural group can prune itself of what is anachronistic and self-defeating, keeping, as Malamud so abundantly shows, only what gives color and flavor, in the deepest sense *vitality*, to life?

Well, in the past hour the opening salvo has been sounded. Perhaps after two other presentations tomorrow and the panel on Sunday morning we may think we will have—if not some answers, at least better comprehension of the questions.

Lester Wolfson receives the honorary degree of Doctor of Humane Letters at 1988 IU South Bend Commencement, from the 15th IU President, Thomas Ehrlich

Index

K

Keats, John (English poet) 47, 53, 54, 73, 74, 75, 76, 110, 135, 136, 138, 166
Kennedy, John F. (American President) 72, 105, 107
Kerr, Clark 1, 7
Keyser, Robert L. 98
King, Martin Luther, Jr. (American civil rights leader) 72, 105
Kozol, Jonathan 100

L

Laudeman, Kent (IUSB Registrar) 185
Lehman, Charles P. 98
Lewis, C. S. (novelist and critic) 68, 74, 107, 165, 193, 195
Lil' Abner 55
Love, Eugene E. 99

M

Mailer, Norman 52
Malamud, Bernard (American author) 54, 74, 76, 209-227
McCormack, Richard and Margaret 58
Menninger, Karl 101
Michael Novak, theologian 101
Millay, Edna St. Vincent (American poet and playwright) 54
Montaigne, Michel de (French Renaissance writer) 71, 171, 176
Morrow, Dr. Joseph E. 99

N

Newman, John Henry, Cardinal 54, 74, 106, 152, 153, 174, 175, 188
Nixon, Richard 93, 113–118
Notre Dame 13, 16, 20, 48, 49, 66, 163, 167

O

Oliphent, Bernadine (Music) 56
Oliver Corporation 48

P

Palumbo, Edward M. 99
Peck, John (Business) 14, 130, 139
    Peck Committee (1971-2) 14
Pepperdine, Warren (Theater) 10, 58, 162
Perrin, Kenneth (Chancellor, IUSB 1997-2005) 35

(and the) civil rights movement 51, 72
(and the) importance of quality graduate research 52
(and the) limits of faculty influence 65
　　　Promotion & Tenure Committee 65
(and the) Penetralium of mystery 75, 136, 142
(and the) social polarization over the Vietnam War 67
(and the) Vietnam War 50, 51, 67, 72, 73, 103, 113
(and the) Wolfson Literary Awards 58, 77
(and) wider vision of educational requirements 70
arrival in South Bend in 1964 9, 94
　　　a university "becoming" 48
celebrates Don Quixote 51, 221
"center of consciousness" 47
degree programs in the liberal arts and sciences 9
enthusiastic advocate for computer science 15
envisioned a small-scale university 8
first speech to the faculty, Sept. 1964 83
his abiding love of the academy 49
his education 48
his many literary allusions and references 49
his youth in Grand Rapids, MI 48, 52
idea of the university as an academic and cultural community 46
IUSB only regional campus with liberal arts core 49
Legacy at IUSB 34
　　　groundbreaking for the Schurz Library 34
Master Plan for the South Bend-Mishawaka Campus, 1966 1, 13
rejects "high visibility" sports 49, 89
support for music, drama, art ix, 6, 8, 12, 13, 37, 46, 49, 51, 54, 55,
　　57, 65, 70, 71, 73, 74, 88, 102, 131-133, 140-142, 150, 179, 184, 195,
　　226
"What's it all about, Alfie?" 45, 76
Wordsworth, William (English poet) 53, 54, 59, 72, 73, 86, 130, 167

Z

Zisla, Harold (Fine Arts) 49, 63, 71